Known only as ADAM, the author
is a young and incredibly gifted
distant-energy healer.

Also by Adam

DreamHealer: A True Story of Miracle Healings

The Path of the DreamHealer

DreamHealer 2

A Guide to Healing
and Self-Empowerment

ADAM

sphere

SPHERE

This edition published in Great Britain in 2006 by Sphere
First published by DreamHealer Inc. in 2004
Published by Penguin Group (Canada), a division of Pearson
Penguin Canada Inc., in 2006

DreamHealer 2 © DreamHealer Inc., 2003, 2006
DreamHealer ™ is a Trademark of DreamHealer Inc.
Visit Adam's website at www.dreamhealer.com for information on workshops
and ordering *DreamHealer* DVDs

The moral right of the author has been asserted.

This publication contains the opinions and ideas of its author and is designed to
provide useful advice in regard to the subject matter covered. This publication is
not intended to provide a basis for action in particular circumstances without
consideration by a competent professional. Your doctor should be consulted for
any medical conditions noted in this book. The visualizations are NOT meant
to replace advice from your health care professional. The author and publisher
expressly disclaim any responsibility for any liability, loss of risk, personal or
otherwise that is incurred as a consequence, direct or indirectly, of the use
and application of any of the contents of this book.

A CIP catalogue record for this book is available from the British Library.

ISBN-13: 978-0-7515-3843-4
ISBN-10: 0-7515-3843-4

Typeset in Minion by M Rules
Printed and bound in Great Britain by
Clays Ltd, St Ives plc

Sphere
An imprint of
Little, Brown Book Group
Brettenham House
Lancaster Place
London WC2E 7EN

A member of the Hachette Livre Group of Companies

www.littlebrown.co.uk

You have the rest of your life to change your future.

—ADAM

Contents

Acknowledgments

Thank you Ivan Rados, for all the effort and dedication you have put into the art for this book. When we first discussed the illustrations required, it didn't take long to come to the realization that some of them were too complex for me to explain to you in words. You suggested that I telepathically send images. I thought this might work because it is one of the techniques I use to help people in comas. I telepathically send them images of familiar people, places or things.

Your intuitive ability has enabled you to receive the information I sent you, and your extraordinary talent, creativity and true artistic vision have created images that closely resemble what I had envisioned.

Thanks Ivan, for giving this book illustrations that go far beyond my stick-man level of art.

Acknowledgements

Also many thanks to Dr. Doris Lora, who encouraged me throughout the writing of this book.

Most of all, thanks to everyone whom I have had the pleasure of meeting when our paths have crossed.

The Journey Continues

I have always been able to see and feel energy fields around humans and all living things. What I didn't realize for many years is that not everyone else can. One day I was drawn to help my mom, who was in agonizing pain from trigeminal neuralgia, an affliction caused by her multiple sclerosis. Without being aware of what I was doing, I took her pain away. Now years later, what was a frequent symptom for her has never returned. Thus, my healing journey began.

The view of the external aura provides useful information about a person's state of health, but I do not use this with what I do. When I perform a healing, I am able to project holographic images in front of me, which are three-dimensional charts of information emitted by the person. I call this "going into" the person because I am able to "go into" their energetic hologram, to directly access their holographic information. This can be accomplished when I am physically with a person, or through a connection made by looking at a photograph. From these holographic views, I can "see" where energy blockages exist and can manipulate energy in the form of information in order to facilitate healing. The person themselves does the healing based on the information they receive.

It doesn't matter how many miles separate us physically—distance is not a factor. I can do what I refer to as "distant healing." The ability to do this exists because of our inherent interconnectedness to each other and to everything else in our universe. This knowledge is essential for our own expanding consciousness.

Healing is something that we are all capable of doing and increasing our skills in. Our own wellness is the responsibility of each and every one of us. It is with this purpose in mind that I have written *DreamHealer 2: A Guide to Healing and Self-Empowerment*, which includes instructions for visualizations you can use to help balance your own energy system back to wellness.

The purpose of my first book, *DreamHealer,* was twofold: to tell the story of the discovery of my healing ability and, more importantly, to help people understand that we all have the capacity to heal and be healed. Soon after the publication of *DreamHealer,* I became aware that many people needed more information on the powerful influence that we all have on our own health and healing. Readers were enthusiastic but often puzzled. They expressed doubts about their own abilities to heal themselves. They peppered me with questions about how to heal.

This second book, *DreamHealer 2: A Guide to Healing and Self-Empowerment,* is an effort to answer that need. It also has a twofold purpose: to provide detailed information on how each of us can heal ourselves and others and, as a result, to address the enormous need for healing on our planet.

Since the release of *DreamHealer,* I have been contacted by many knowledgeable and enlightened people with messages of encouragement and support. I also received thousands of emails from individuals in need of healing. Some contacts were desperate pleas for help from people who lacked a basic understanding or knowledge of the connection we all share. In this book, I discuss at length our connections with each other and with universal energy.

Many requests for healing have been heart wrenching beyond words. I have been confronted by people who are at the end of their rope and "willing to try anything." I have been asked to quit high school, friends and hobbies to allow for more time to heal others. One fellow even suggested I sleep less. Even if I were healing 24–7, there would not be enough time to address all these needs. This book is a step in the direction of meeting that need.

As a healer, I must always be aware of how much energy I can give to others and how much to reserve for myself. Consider this parable: There was once a healer in New Zealand who became famous. He had been an alcoholic, but his life took a turn when he discovered his ability to heal. People came from far and wide seeking his help. There was always a lineup of people stretching from his front door far down the street. For several years, he gave to others all the help he possibly could, while sacrificing his own needs. Then one day he collapsed under the awesome responsibility that healing brings with it. He took up drinking again as an escape. He never healed again.

Every healer knows this to be true: Give of yourself, but *always* save lots for yourself. Maintain your own life, your own interests and the space you need. In doing so, you can remain devoted to helping others.

It is clear that with a world population of approximately six billion, we need millions of healers. My goal is to teach as many people as possible, since everything we need to heal ourselves is already within us. We just need the tools to effectively tap into the mind–immune system connection and use it to heal. Teaching effective healing tools is the focus of *DreamHealer 2: A Guide to Healing and Self-Empowerment*. With this book, I hope to assist in empowering millions of people to become self-healers.

HEALING IS A CHOICE

All healing is participatory, no matter what the method. Even Western medicine, which is allopathic—

dealing with disease with treatments, including drugs, that have the opposite effect to the symptoms—accepts the idea that patients must be willing to improve their own health in order for their health to improve.

Many people have been encouraged to leave all the responsibility for their wellness in someone else's hands, usually a medical authority. Each of us must realize that we ultimately choose every aspect of our health care. We are in charge. In this way, we become our own masters; we claim our birthright of total self-empowerment. At every turning point in life, there are decisions which we make ourselves. We define and create our own futures. Our wellness—physical, emotional and spiritual—is part of this creation.

It is our choice whether we smoke, drink, take drugs, worry or place unnecessary stress or risk in our lives. Each lifestyle choice has consequences, but we ultimately make the decision. Generally, people want to remove themselves from the responsibility of their illnesses. They tend to pass that responsibility on to someone else, particularly to a healer such as myself. However, everyone must understand that healing themselves is ultimately their responsibility.

When people tell me that they will leave their healing in my hands, I have a serious discussion with them. I will not do a treatment on anyone who doesn't accept the participatory nature of healing. The healer does not do the healing directly. The healer simply creates an efficient connection in order to facilitate the healing.

We also have other choices that influence our health. We can choose to ignore our own energy systems or we can dedicate time to understanding them. A healthy energy flow pattern will help each of us. To achieve this, everyone should strive to maximize his or her potential. When you are being your best self, the positive energy will radiate out in waves of healing that will affect everyone and everything, well beyond your conscious awareness.

Chapter I
Accepting Responsibility

The most powerful tool to heal yourself is yourself.

—ADAM

What is the most extensive untapped resource in modern medicine? It is the power of every person to heal himself. Millions of people put the responsibility of their personal health care in the hands of others. In many cases, the underlying cause is rarely dealt with. I challenge you to take charge of your own health. Make sure that your lifestyle choices are healthy ones. Accept the primary responsibility for maintaining your health. After all, no one is more interested in your health than you are. Learn about your body and how to avoid illness.

Your best defense against illness is your immune system working at its optimum level. What you think directly affects the efficacy of your immune system. Do some research so you can make educated decisions about what is best for you. For instance, if you have a pancreatic problem, get an anatomy book and learn where the pancreas is located, what it looks like and how it works. Learn everything that you can about the pancreas. Then you can use this knowledge when you do the visualizations I outline in this book, making them much easier to do and more effective.

Set new intentions to counter old habits. Habits play a part in reinforcing behavior. They can strengthen our resolve through positive habits but can also intensify problems through negative thoughts and beliefs. Because of their routine nature, they are counterproductive to positive change within yourself. Only you can change yourself. All true and permanent change comes from within. Understand that in order to improve your well-being, you must first believe that this is possible. The following three statements illustrate the progression necessary to bring your belief system in line with the possibilities of self-healing.

1. I can be well again (possible)
2. I will be well again (probable)
3. I am well again (being well)

Wellness involves looking carefully at your lifestyle: at your habits, attitudes and emotions. Those seeking better health must have a true desire to reach the goal of being well.

THE ROLE OF HABITS

In many illnesses, the individual's habits are a contributing factor. The first step to healing yourself is examining your habits and practices from a non-biased, or objective, point of view. Recall everything that you did today that may have had a negative impact on your health. If you are having difficulty doing this, ask a close friend or relative who knows you well. Ask that person to tell you honestly how she thinks you could improve your lifestyle.

It may be more difficult to recognize an underlying negative lifestyle factor, such as stress, than a more obvious poor choice, such as smoking. Changing your lifestyle for the better can have only a positive impact, so it is essential to have the willpower and discipline to make the necessary changes.

This approach to analyzing your lifestyle involves not only becoming aware of negative aspects that are causing problems but focusing on those that will create a positive impact in your life. Make all your choices healthy ones. Decide what habits and practices you must change and take the appropriate action to change them. Take control of this power that you have to change any unhealthy habits and, consequently, your life. This amounts to only a fraction of the incredible potential of self-empowerment at your disposal.

I have received many emails from people seeking help who have lung-related diseases, only to learn that they are still smoking. If they cannot throw away the cigarettes, do they sincerely have the desire to get better and heal themselves?

It would be unwise to spend my time and energy helping someone who refuses to make such changes and continues the behavior that may have caused or at least contributed to the problem in the first place.

The desire to take positive steps for your health is the same desire that will empower you to get better. The healer points the body in the right direction for healing: It is *you* who must continue in that direction. It is your body, so take care of it. You are ultimately in charge.

THE ROLE OF ATTITUDES

The second step toward self-healing is creating a positive social environment that will enhance your healing ability. The attitudes of those around you have a huge effect on your well-being. Therefore, not only must you change your habits, diet and thought patterns, but you must influence people around you to change their attitudes and be more positive. When those around you observe your efforts to improve your own health, many will radiate positive thoughts. When you and all the people around you are thinking positively, you are creating a perfect healing environment and increasing the effectiveness of your healing process. Conversely, when people around you are always negative, their negative attitudes interfere with and counter your positive healing process.

Be aware of the impact that other people's thoughts and attitudes have on you and your well-being. Make mental notes about when you feel best and in whose company. The choice is ultimately yours as to what energy you expose yourself to. You are responsible not only for your own attitudes but also for those that you allow to influence your own. Surround yourself with positive, like-minded people.

Negativity is the most common attitude problem that people face today. Your positive outlook will guide you hand in hand with your physical recovery. Everyone must put his past difficulties behind him. The past is past; you cannot change it. You can only change your present, which impacts your future possibilities.

Imagine two people in the hospital with identical illnesses. One believes and so is thinking that he is getting better and will be home in a few days. The other believes his illness is going to be with him for-ever and is thinking that he will probably never leave the hospital alive. Which of the two will recover faster? The positive person, of course. We have all had the pleasure of meeting these people in life who accept any challenge with a positive expectation of outcome. And guess what? Good things *do* happen to them. The power of thought cannot be overestimated.

All thoughts and intentions radiate throughout the universe. Everything is connected to everything else because the universe is composed only of energy. Thought or intention is a form of energy; therefore, every intention you have radiates out forever, affecting everything in its path. It is like a ripple in a pond. Every molecule in the pond is affected to some degree by that ripple.

Start today by having a positive outlook from this day forth. See the glass as being half full, not half empty. In any situation there is always hope. Be the optimist. This positive attitude is essential to the success of your healing.

It helps enormously to have a regular companion with you while doing the visualization techniques that are explained in the upcoming chapters. If someone close to you has the same common intention and visualization, the effect of that intention will be greatly amplified.

Finally, cultivate an attitude of open-mindedness. Many people are skeptical of what they cannot perceive with their five senses. A popular children's book says in its wisdom that everything important can be seen with the heart, which is, of course, invisible to the eyes. In this way, we must look beyond our familiar paradigms and keep an open mind about that which we cannot see. Always remember that a closed mind can be locked only from the inside. It therefore follows that a closed mind can be unlocked only from the inside, too.

Wellness involves an open, positive, responsible and participatory attitude toward one's own well-being. The old parable about giving a man a fish versus teaching him to fish nicely explains the participation required in any healing: Give a man a fish, and you feed him for a day. Teach a man to fish, and he feeds himself for life. Teach him how to make a fishing rod, and he will teach his children how to make them.

Giving a man a fish is like the healer healing a

person without any participation on the part of the healee. The expectation on the part of the healee is sometimes referred to as the magic wand syndrome: No participation is required. No change in lifestyle is expected, and there is no need to reflect on how the illness occurred. A totally passive relationship is created. The healer provides what is needed, and the healee gives away the responsibility for his own health.

On the other hand, teaching a man to fish requires two-way participation, just as with healing. The healer gives instructions on how to participate in one's own wellness. Both healer and healee understand that healing is a two-way process. The healer's responsibility is to examine the lifestyle, stress and emotional responses that led the person to this point and to suggest the necessary changes that will prevent health problems from reoccurring or continuing. It is understood that this is a lifetime challenge that requires constant attention in order to affect permanent change. A participatory relationship leads to lasting changes in health.

However, teaching a man how to make a fishing

rod ensures he has a lifelong tool. Similarly, the healer teaches the healee the concept of self-healing and maintaining a state of wellness. Consequently, the healee achieves a state of complete self-empowerment. Total responsibility is with the healee, as he handcrafts his own fishing rod or state of health. A creative process has been achieved.

Ideally, people should understand the dynamics of the healing process completely so that they can improve the design for maximum efficiency for themselves. People should understand that the ability to re-create their reality lies within each and every one of us. Accessing this ability requires imagination and a sense of knowing this to be true, based on personal experience.

When the healee achieves a firm understanding of the healing modality, he is then able to teach others. This should be the ultimate goal of both the healer and healee.

THE ROLE OF EMOTIONS
Emotional problems are usually very complex and, in many situations, they develop into physical prob-

lems. Often we let emotions dictate our subconscious intentions and, therefore, our wellness. If you master the control of your emotions, you are in control of your immune system and thus your health.

To master our emotions, we should practice tuning in to ourselves in order to understand what makes us tick. What more worthwhile endeavor could there possibly be in this lifetime than to develop a deeper appreciation of ourselves? We can start by being aware of what pushes our buttons. What situations drive us to distraction? What characteristics in others drive us crazy? What triggers our positive and negative emotional responses, which in turn flood our systems with energy? Only when we understand what makes us tick can we set out to control these reactions.

It has long been established in all types of medicine that emotions play a major role in the efficacy of our immune systems. Listen to what you tell yourself; notice what replays in your mind. Is this working toward your own good, or is it providing negative reinforcement? The good must be given every opportunity to flourish. What you don't need must not be given the strength and resources it needs to exist. You don't need it, so get rid of it.

Visualize cleaning your room and throwing out all of the old, unused stuff—broken items, stray parts of things whose origins you have long since forgotten. Be thorough and selective. Keep only what you need to help you achieve the goal of re-creating your new positive reality.

This housecleaning of your past is necessary in order for you to understand what you have experienced, how you have interpreted those experiences and what emotional baggage needs to be addressed. It is like eliminating the junk emails from your computer. If you don't do this on a regular basis, your entire system slows down, becoming less efficient and eventually dysfunctional.

Habitual emotional responses are difficult to change. An established pattern creates a tape loop of sorts in the mind, going around and around on the same circuit. Break the pattern and move on, as it is detrimental to your health. Understand that your happiness is not dependent on what happens to you and around you, but how you process things within you. Your emotions depend on what you think, and you control your thoughts.

Life is for learning. What better goal could we have than to learn as much about ourselves as we can in this lifetime? Through learning about how we react to various situations, we also develop the ability to relate to others in a more meaningful and compassionate way. This new state of awareness sends out ripples of positive energy. Our concept of self, or "me," becomes more connected to everyone and everything around us. Improving the energy balance of one person ultimately affects us all.

Chapter 2
The Living Aura

*The harmonious flow of one's energy
defines one's health pattern.*

—ADAM

*E*very living organism emits an energy field, which is visible to many people in the form of light. This energy field is commonly referred to as an aura. The aura is a reflection of the organism's intentions and its physical and emotional structure. This aura surrounds every living thing. The physical structure of the organism appears to influence the manner in which the energy flows. The auras around plants appear to be colorless and look like heat waves shimmering and rising from a hot road in summer. In humans, an aura looks like a bubble of swirling colored waves.

I know many of us are born with the ability to

see auras because when I change mine in front of a baby—by projecting it above my head, for instance—the baby's eyes tend to follow the change. But this ability gets suppressed as we grow up. It is not something that is accepted in Western society, so over time people lose this ability, whether deliberately or not. With a little practice, we can retrain ourselves to see auras.

A person's aura is like a fingerprint or genetic marker that uniquely identifies the individual. Twins can be genetically identical yet their auras look completely different. No two auras are alike. They differ in color, intensity, size and shape. Emotions seem to influence change in the aura's color. People are always interested in what colors their auras are. However, I don't see the value of categorizing aura colors into "red means this and blue means that." The important aspect is the dynamic, harmonious flow of energy.

THE AURA OF A HEALTHY BODY

In a state of good physical health, a person's aura looks like an ocean of colors flowing around the body; there is harmonious flow of color throughout the aura as the colors smoothly transition from one to another. The manner in which a person's energy flows outside and inside her body is a unique identifier of the individual. Some people have a translucent flowing energy near the surface of the body. Others have another brighter layer that contains colors of swirling energy. Some people have lots of colors in their auras and others have very little color. Some auras extend well beyond the body, and others barely extend beyond the physical body. The same person's aura can appear very different under different conditions, depending, for example, on the degree of emotional stress.

These observations have taught me that the most important aspect of a person's aura is how it flows. Harmonious flow of one's energy defines one's health pattern. A splatter painting may contain exactly the same paint and materials as the *Mona Lisa;* the difference is in the pattern in which the materials are applied. A symphony being practiced by an orchestra may contain all the same notes as the perfected performance; the difference is in which notes are played with others. Harmony or coherence, in these examples, is what distinguishes chaos from order.

As a problem begins to develop, the energy begins to lose this harmony. The energy in the aura near the problem becomes stagnant. All the cells in a person's body are working in unison and share an interconnectedness to each other; therefore, a change in one cell affects all the others.

None of us has a perfectly healthy body. We all have something that causes breaks to show up in our auras, whether it is an old injury, an existing ailment, or a developing issue. Re-establishing this harmonious flow gives each of us a goal to constantly work toward. Many people have the ability to see these auras with varying degrees of intensity and can easily determine where a problem exists in the body.

The external auric view of the physical body gives me a broad perspective and is a good indicator of general problems in the body. When the problem is deeper within the body, I have to be able to see the body's inner energies to cause lasting change. I do this by connecting to the person's quantum hologram.

In order to understand the quantum science, there are some basic quantum concepts you need to wrap your mind around. In the quantum world of subatomic particles, a quantum object such as an electron can exist at more than one place at a time. Until we actually observe it as a particle, it behaves unlike our perception of space-time reality. It seemingly moves from one site to another without moving between the two locations. Rather than being like motion as we know it, the process is more like disappearing from one place and reappearing elsewhere. This is referred to as the quantum leap.

Quantum physics also explains how someone's holographic information can be accessed and influenced from anywhere, making distance not a factor, and therefore distant healing possible. Information about everyone and everything is intertwined, or interconnected. On a subatomic level, one quantum object simultaneously influences a correlated twin object no matter how far apart they are. This is called quantum action-at-a-distance and is the basis of nonlocality phenomena, including distant healing. For decades, physicists have shown this—it is no longer just theoretical.

Every physical object emits its own quantum hologram, or information, that contains all past, present and future data. All particles are fundamentally connected to all other particles. I see this field of quantum information as a web, or network, of pathways connecting everything to everything else. This is what I am able to access when I do an energy healing on someone.

During a treatment, I project holographic images, or holograms, in front of me. If the person is not physically with me, I use her photograph to make a connection to her. Holograms are the visual guidance, like three-dimensional maps, that appear before me when I am viewing someone for treatment. All the body's information is available in this manner. From this field of quantum information, I can focus or zoom in using specific information or views, which I project as a hologram.

When I go into someone and access her hologram,

I can effectively tune in to various subsets of information. It's kind of like changing channels on the television. My mind acts as the remote control, which adjusts to a different set of frequencies, thus giving me different holographic views of the person's health data. These subsets or layers of information become visually accessible to me. For example, I am able to see the nervous, musculo-skeletal and energetic systems as well as the organs. Selecting a particular body system is similar to looking at a computer screen. My thought or intention is the cursor click on the screen that accesses the information I need.

Once this holographic information appears before me, I can manipulate the energy so that the person can find her way back to a healthy state. People who have observed me doing this tell me that it looks as though I am conducting an orchestra. My arms and hands wave through the air, and my fingers nimbly create patterns as I make energy adjustments. To the observer it appears to be mesmerizing yet patterned flowing gestures, like the dancing of flames in a raging fire. Through intentions of healing, I provide information to the person

I am treating. I do this by being in resonance with the person's body. This means that the frequency that we are tuned to is similar.

In this way, the body of the person is interacting and exchanging information with me. This stimulates the healee to energetically alter her state of wellness, which is in turn reflected in her hologram, as intentions manipulate the shape of the aura. I can usually see this change starting to take place immediately. Everyone's body knows its own way back to wellness; it just needs some guidance. These specific adjustments to the energy system help the body achieve this.

Think of this process as similar to an architect viewing blueprints of a proposed renovation. The existing building is physically in front of you. The vision of the future or your goal or plan is what you must visualize in your mind's eye. Each future view can be seen on the blueprint.

During a treatment, I redirect the energy flow on the hologram in accordance with the body's optimum state. At each stage between this perfect vision and the present health situation, adjustment and time are required. The problem must be removed, just as in a renovation. Most importantly, both you and the healer must keep the vision of the desired end result in your mind's eye.

Some of the holographic images I see are more useful than others in viewing certain problems, just as some blueprints reveal certain details more clearly than others. The electrical blueprint is needed for accessing certain information, while the floor plan is more useful for other aspects. But all are needed in order to complete the renovation.

THE AURA OF ILLNESS

If someone has an illness or injury, I see the problem as varying shades of green energy inside the body. This sluggish energy has lost its direction. I refer to these areas as energy blockages. With different visualization techniques, I can eliminate these energy blockages and return the body to a state of wellness. While I am doing this, my intuition usually allows me to pick up other related information that may help me to more efficiently redirect the person's energy so that it in turn is flowing more efficiently.

Many illnesses have specific appearances, or signatures, that define them. Fibromyalgia and chronic fatigue syndrome show up as a hypersensitivity of the nerve endings, so I use the nervous system hologram to view these. Multiple sclerosis looks like grains of green sand bubbling up from the base of the spine and collecting in the brain. Organs that have problems have a cloudy ring around them. Cancer has a unique, radiating green glow to it. With experience, I am learning how to more effectively and efficiently do this specific energy work. Each healing is part of an ongoing learning experience.

The auras that I saw in my high school's crowded hallways were overwhelming. I sometimes needed my girlfriend to guide me down the hall, as the auras were overpowering my vision. I found it challenging to see while navigating through the hallway. For this reason, I made the conscious decision to turn down the auras, as they were far too much information for me to process. Once again, trying something new was an amazing learning experience for me. After I consciously turned down the intensity of the auras I was seeing, I found that I received far more intuitive information than before. This basically saves me a step, as I don't need to interpret visual input, which I receive in the form of auras. I can bypass this step and access the information directly.

Our pattern of wellness is like a coiled spring. If you pull the spring out and let it go, it will return to its original shape. It is quite flexible and forgiving. However, if you pull it too often, the spring eventually will stay in its stretched shape. Our objective should be to stretch that spring as infrequently as possible. By maintaining our health, we won't risk stretching ourselves beyond our limitations to rebound back to our healthy state.

The following are five main points about the aura:

- An aura is flowing energy and changes color constantly.
- Every living thing has a unique aura.
- Auras vary in intensity in different people.
- An injury or illness shows up as a break in the aura.

- In perfect health, the colors of the aura are bright and the flow is unimpeded and harmonious.

ENERGY EXERCISES

The following exercises will help you develop your skills in feeling and seeing your own energy, and then bringing in universal energy to your body.

I. Feel Your Energy

1. Rub your palms together in a circular motion. Feel the generation of heat. This is your own energy.
2. Now hold your hands about two inches apart, palm to palm. Push your hands toward one another without actually moving them. That is, visualize your hands pushing toward one another. Feel the resistance, similar to two like magnets repelling each other.
3. Spread your hands varying distances apart and feel the same resistance.
4. Establish the threshold distance at which your palms can be separated and you still feel your

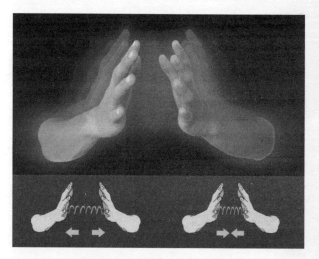

Illustration 1: Feel your energy

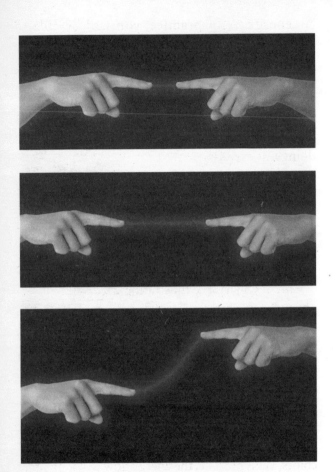

Illustration 2: See your energy

energy. With practice, you will be able to increase this distance as you become more sensitive to energy.

Illustration 1 depicts both the energy around your hands and the resistance you should feel when doing this exercise.

2. See Your Energy

1. Against a dark background, hold your hands in front of you with your fingertips pointing to the fingertips of the other hand, about two inches apart (see Illustration 2).
2. Move your fingers slowly up and down and in and out. Think about the energy flowing from one fingertip to the other. You will see a faint line of energy passing between them. At first this may appear as a hazy band.

Practice this exercise against backgrounds of various colors. With practice, the energy flow will look more defined.

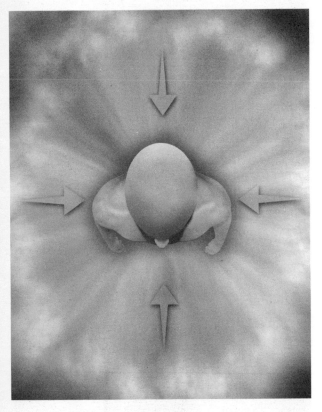

Illustration 3:
Bird's-eye view of bringing in universal energy

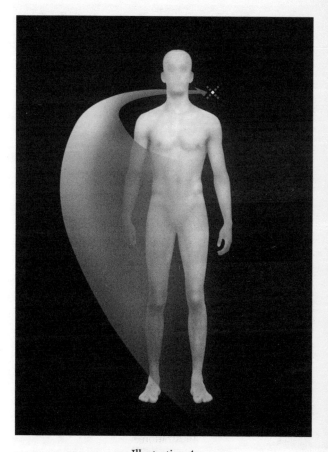

Illustration 4:
Seeing an aura:
Focus on a spot behind the person

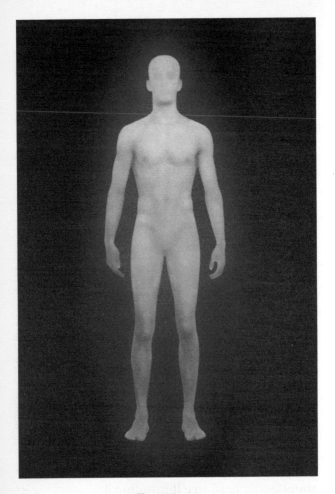

Illustration 5:
A slight, shimmering aura

3. Bring in Universal Energy

1. Imagine all the energy of the universe circling above your head, available for your use.

2. Bring in energy through the top of your head and collect it in your heart area.

3. Send the energy from the heart area down through your right arm, through your right fingertips, back into your left fingers and up through your left arm and to the heart.

4. Continue to imagine this flow as an energy circuit; from your heart to right arm, right hand, right fingertips, to left fingertips, left arm and then to the heart.

At first you may see just a faint line. With practice, you will be surprised at how quickly you will see defined energy flow. (See Illustration 3.)

4. How to See a Person's Aura

Look past the person whose aura you want to see. Concentrate on an area about two inches above his shoulders or head (see Illustration 4).

At first you may see a slight shimmering aura,

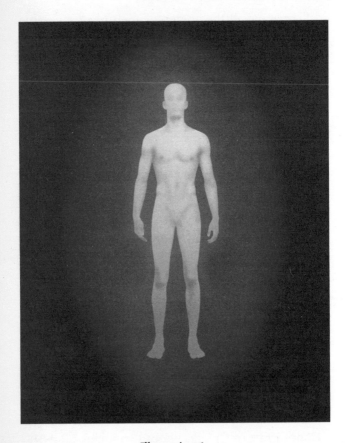

Illustration 6:
An aura with defined flowing colors

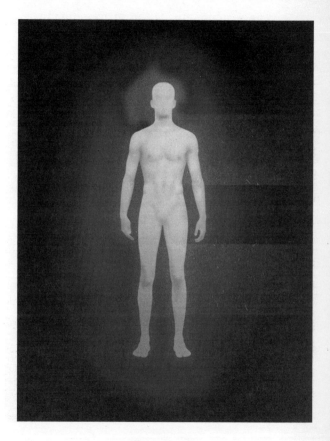

Illustration 7:
A break in the aura, in the head area

similar to the one shown in Illustration 5. The aura may appear as a faint emanation surrounding material objects. Some people describe this as similar to heat waves, others as a misty fog. It will likely be far easier to see the aura after you've done a treatment using the visualizations discussed in this book. Few people will see the aura with the color intensity shown in Illustration 6, but with practice, you may see the defined flowing colors. Keep practicing!

5. Energy Flow Representation

A body without injury or illness would have harmonious energy flow. A body developing an injury or illness has energy that is beginning to lose its path or direction. A body with a fully developed injury or illness has a break in the energy flow, as depicted in Illustration 7, and can't find its way back to a harmonious energy flow, or wellness. Here is an advanced exercise to see energy flow; keep it in mind as a long-term goal.

1. Stand in front of a full-length mirror.
2. Relax your eyes.

3. Practice seeing and feeling your own energy flow.

Try doing this in both light and dark conditions. You can do this exercise with another person as well, practicing to see each other's energy flow. At first, you may be guided primarily by intuition—by feeling the energy. Soon you will be able to see it as well. As you develop this skill, you will find that your intuitive sense increases along with your healing ability. Trust that you can do this.

What do you experience when you connect to another person's hologram?

To connect to a person I look at a photograph of him and then rapidly connect to him through his eyes. Everything in the room I'm in goes dark and then I see three-dimensional images of the person in front of me, laid out before me like charts of information. While connected to someone, I pick up a great deal of intuitive information also. For instance, I am often keenly aware of a person's attitude stemming from his belief system. I feel whether a person is sincerely interested in pursuing this type of treatment. I just get a strong sense of knowing, but it is not necessarily from anything I saw. I also get a deep sense of interconnectedness.

How do you explain the idea in distant healing that distance is not a factor?

Many people have great difficulty accepting that a person's health can be influenced from a distance. Yet, my healing is done with intention, which is not restricted by distance at all. Science has many sound explanations for our interconnectedness to each other and how the intentions of one affect another instantly, regardless of the distance between us. This is explained in quantum physics mainly by the phenomenon of quantum nonlocality, where a change to one object instantly influences its correlated twin object, regardless of distance.

Many people can accept how someone can be healed when within arm's reach of a healer but cannot understand how this could work from farther away. There is no distance at which the healing will be ineffectual. The idea that distance is a factor is simply a paradigm that develops from living in our Newtonian physics–based everyday reality. When doing distant healing, we are operating beyond the material limitations on objects being either here *or* there in time and space. Information is present at all times and all places simultaneously.

Chapter 3
The Mind–Body Connection

The subconscious mind is molded by what we tell ourselves.

—ADAM

Illustration 8:
Your mind directly affects your immune system

THE IMMUNE SYSTEM

People tend to think of the mind and the immune system as two unrelated entities. Yet, you were born with an integral connection between the mind and the immune system as a natural self-defense mechanism. The mind directly influences the immune system. The mind is the command center. Illustration 8 is a portrayal of how all things are interconnected. When the mind is sending helpful signals to enhance the proper functioning of the immune system, the immune system in turn allows for a healthier functioning mind. This is why it is important to always keep the relationship depicted in Illustration 8 in mind.

When you are injured, your mind is subconsciously directing the immune system to heal the injured area. Your immune system responds by initiating various chemical reactions where needed. For instance, you don't have to think about healing a cut on your finger. The healing occurs automatically.

Your goal in self-healing is to reach this level of control over your immune system on a conscious level. We all have that ability and can learn to direct it consciously for more serious problems. There is an increasing number of medical studies confirming the mind's ability to control the immune system. This is the key to the process of self-healing and to maximizing its benefits.

From conception until birth, each of us had a vital connection to another being, as we all shared every necessity of life with our mothers while in the womb. This bond was our first experience of totally being at one with another physical person, where every breath of air, every bite of food and every feeling is shared. When I look at expectant mothers, I can see their baby reacting to the mom's energy pattern. A happy mom sends harmonious healthy energy flowing to her baby. A happy mom is a happy baby.

AWARENESS OF CHILDREN

At birth, our own mind–body connection is complete. Every cell understands its connection to every other cell, and they all function as one.

It is common knowledge that salamanders have the capacity to regenerate a severed limb. A medical fact that most people don't know is that humans have a similar ability until around the age of twelve. If a child has a finger cut off up to the first knuckle, the missing portion will regenerate within ninety days. The energetic patterns of our DNA mobilize to rebuild the missing part. What is even more amazing is that there is no scientific explanation for this. Surely this phenomenon warrants more attention and investigation.

What we do know is that the genetic memory of the complete finger apparently still exists within one's energy field. Why is it that children are able to tap into this effectively until the age of around twelve, and then the ability disappears? One reason may be that children's boundaries of "possible" and "impossible" are not yet well defined. For them, psychic and mystical experiences, extrasensory perception (ESP) and seeing auras are everyday events. It's just that these phenomena have never been discussed.

I had the pleasure of doing workshops with kids at the International Healing Gathering in Saskatchewan, Canada. Most were Native, and had a cultural appreciation of our energetic connection. All were younger than eighteen. During my demonstrations to show energy, they all could clearly see the energy right away. One kid exclaimed, "Oh, that's what that is!" The others nodded in agreement. They had not yet been taught that seeing energy is impossible. They still experienced all events as being equally valid.

Over time, this open state of mind and unlimited expectation is taught out of us. The seeing of energy is beyond the boundaries of our acceptable reality and is dismissed and not discussed. We are told there is a time and place for such science fiction notions and nonreality-based possibilities, separate from everyday life.

Children expect nothing more in life than to experience everything to the fullest. They are excited about what each new day may bring and meet it with radiating self-confidence and a readiness to learn new things. As we get older, we adopt the cultural view of ourselves as separate from everyone and everything else in the physical world. Our "me" ideas develop. We are taught one set of expectations for our minds and another for our bodies. Our minds are supposed to achieve academic excellence at school. Our bodies are expected to grow strong independently of our minds.

Before I entered school, I thought that I was artistic. Then I met kids whose doodling looked like the drawings in professional comic strips. My opinion of my artistic abilities plummeted. Every one of us has experienced this shattering of our self-confidence at one time or another. It is vital that we get this back.

At school and in our leisure time, we compete

with each other mentally (through academics) or physically (through sports). This is how we learn to view ourselves, and how others relate to us. We become known for our traits and become labeled: the runner, the nerd, the loner, the popular kid.

REINTEGRATION OF SELF

Society has placed perceived but artificial boundaries on each of us. The fragmented self can be reversed so that we function as integrated beings. In reality, we are one with ourselves and one with everything. Our consciousness and the universal consciousness is an interconnection of constant information exchange. Some day, a truth as obvious as this won't have to be seen as a self-revelation but instead will be readily accepted.

Subconscious and conscious thoughts should work together to achieve the same goal of wellness. The subconscious mind is molded by what we tell ourselves and what we physically do. It should be focused on the goal of maximizing wellness, and this focus must be constantly reinforced.

Our subconscious thoughts and background

self-talk are equally powerful for wellness and should be synchronized with the conscious mind. The conscious mind influences the subconscious mind, and the subconscious mind is at one with the immune system. As a result, your conscious intentions have an effect on your immune system.

The most efficient way to direct the immune system through the mind is through visualizations at or near your sleep state. You are closest to your subconscious mind when you are sleeping or in a relaxed or meditative state.

When awake, make sure that you are constantly reinforcing positive thoughts toward others and yourself—and toward your future self—which you are now in the active state of reinventing. Think of this process as weeding the garden: Keep only what is helpful to you. If what you need flourishes, there is no room for that which you don't need.

When I connect to a person's energy system, I resonate at the frequency of that person in his subconscious healing state. This allows my treatments to usually have a very strong impact on that person's immune system. You can do the same within your own body by understanding the important link between your immune system and your mind, and how it functions as an integrated whole. You have complete control over your conscious and even your subconscious thoughts. Therefore, you also have complete control over your immune system and consequently your health.

For most of us, this thinking requires a paradigm shift. Not only does Western (allopathic) medicine view the body as separate from the mind and spirit, it also separates the body into its anatomical parts, with various medical specialties encompassing each of these parts. There is little or no awareness of the energy body. Every adult needs to relearn what they once knew as children but have since forgotten. Children view people as energetic beings, and as a *whole* being rather than a sum of their parts. This philosophy or vision is the key to our state of wellness. We hold this key. Go with it. Explore it. Enjoy it. Move forward with your new healing attitude.

Why do you think that many people in our society have such difficulty accepting energy treatments?

We are trained from an early age that seeing is believing. This reinforces that what falls beyond the limitations of our five senses should be dismissed and disregarded. Our energetic self and treatment of it challenges what we are taught.

Science has been granted some leeway in this, as most people accept that there are many observations that can be measured by technical equipment yet cannot be seen with the naked eye. The scientific pioneers who initially searched for these invisible effects were doubted—Louis Pasteur, Madame Curie and Nikola Tesla, to name just a few. These scientists not only risked their reputations but endangered their lives in the course of their experiments in order to advance science.

We must accept that many things exist beyond what our five senses can detect. Try seeing from your heart and feeling with your eyes. You may be surprised by what you can learn this way.

How can we assist ourselves in mind–body healing?

In order for mind–body healing to be effective, the healee should view the mind, body and spirit as one. It is impossible to energetically affect one area without influencing all. Every aspect of us and our being is affected by everything else that we think, say and do. Through self-reflection and understanding ourselves we can directly assist ourselves in our healing journey. Be aware of your conscious and subconscious thoughts.

How do I influence my subconscious mind?

The subconscious and the conscious mind are constantly interacting, resulting in a back-and-forth influence. Your conscious thoughts are manifested from your subconscious self. Your conscious experiences are recorded in your subconscious mind, thus influencing your subconscious mind. Because of this interaction, you are able to affect your subconscious thinking. Your subconscious thinking can be changed.

For instance, an alcoholic may find it difficult to quit drinking if he continues to hang out with his old drinking buddies. If he is serious about breaking his addiction, he will find it easier to do so if he is not in a setting that triggers drinking associations for him. By changing his actions and conscious awareness, he is reprogramming his thought patterns, thereby influencing his subconscious.

Chapter 4
Healing Information

You are always the person in charge of your own wellness.

—ADAM

INTUITION

We all have the ability to heal, but not all of us have developed our healing skills. Learning these skills is like anything else we do: It takes practice. There is no doubt that Wayne Gretzky was born with a special ability to play hockey, but he still worked hard to be able to play hockey incredibly well. Many other athletes play great hockey; they just had to work a lot harder at it than Wayne did, and even then they didn't achieve his level of excellence. Nonetheless, their hard work brought results.

In any athletic endeavor, the top athletes depend

on intuition or feel. Perhaps they feel the energy shifts but are unable to actually see them. This is called "anticipating" the opponent's move or "reading" the situation—or simply being "in the zone." It is this awareness of intuitive abilities and being able to use this gift strategically that separates the good athletes from the great ones in any sport.

The same is true in business. All the charts and graphs—the facts—of an economic issue must be interpreted in order to determine a move forward or shape an executive decision. The process of interpretation necessitates the involvement of intuition; that is, how one feels about how events will evolve. Learning to trust your intuition and "go with it" takes practice. The same is true in every aspect of our lives. Trust yourself.

ENERGY CONNECTIONS

The universe is all energy, which is received and interpreted by us as information. This links all of us. Ripples in the energy system are like ripples in a pond: Everyone affects everyone else.

Can you imagine how powerful an influence it

would be if all good news were given front-page status and all bad happenings were relegated to the back pages? Every morning we would awaken to an upbeat connection with each other. The positive intentions would ripple outward and reach everywhere. Don't you wonder why this seems like such a preposterous idea?

I have already, in Chapter 2, briefly covered some principles of quantum physics as they relate to distant healing. At the quantum level, there is no difference between "here" and "there." In quantum physics, this is referred to as nonlocality. The effect we have on each other extends far beyond merely the direct physical contact that we experience with our five senses.

The study of quantum physics has been around for only a hundred years. There are many published reports and studies investigating the major role that quantum physics plays in the energy field in which we live. However, the mere mention of the word "quantum" evokes a mental block of sorts in our minds—kind of like when you say the word "calculus" to high school students. We feel anxiety. It's true that quantum physics is complicated. But there are certain aspects of it—energy as information, for example—that can be explained so that everyone has some understanding of its role in our connectedness.

ENERGY AS INFORMATION

Every physical object emits information in the form of quantum data. We can pick up this information. The body's field of quantum information is accessed and then assessed by the healer. The healer looks at the quantum information of the body in its current state. The healer notices the areas of difficulty. He then sends new information to the person, which facilitates a change in the existing quantum hologram of that person's body. The body's new goal is to update the physical to match the newly accessed quantum information.

This is not as mysterious as it sounds. When we accurately perceive a common event—who is at the door or who is phoning, for instance—we are receiving nonlocal quantum data referred to as intuitive information. This ability can be developed further through practice. We often call this ability our sixth sense. Some people are predisposed to this sixth sense for tuning in to this nonlocal information system.

When I am doing a treatment, I project the three-dimensional image of the person in front of me and change the information through intention. This affects change at the information's source, which in this case is the person's physical body. It is this technique that I am teaching.

The following Seven Steps for Life serve as a great starting point for anyone embarking on a healing journey. These steps should be referred to often and followed as closely as possible. Focus on ways in which you can incorporate them into your everyday life. We are all healers.

SEVEN STEPS FOR LIFE
Step I: Feel Your Own Energy and Be Aware of It
To feel your own energy, rub your palms together in a circle. Be sure to rub the spot right in the center of your palms. Feel the generation of heat. It is your energy. Then hold your palms an inch or two apart

and feel the magnetic push and pull. Move your palms farther apart, until you can no longer feel your energy field. Play with your energy and have fun with it. Our energy system is what this is all about, so become aware of it.

This flow of energy is our life force. It is more important than any other single body system because it involves all of them. Yet, our digestive, respiratory, circulatory, metabolic and nervous systems are better known in Western medicine. We have created lots of tests to measure the efficiency and health level of each of these. But we have yet to develop a measurable level for our energy system, and so it is ignored. Yet, it directly affects all aspects of our health. Learn to feel it, work with it and, most of all, enjoy it.

Step 2: Breathe Abdominally and Be Aware of It

Breathe deeply. Many people usually breathe shallow breaths from their chests and are actually somewhat oxygen deprived. The body gets enough to function, but would function even better with deep, full breaths. Singers and athletes are very aware of how proper breathing enhances their performance. We all need air in order for us to reach our maximum potential. Breathing using your diaphragm and abdominal muscles promotes relaxation and reduces tension.

Breathe in through your nose and imagine filling your abdomen with air. Once full, exhale through your mouth and pull in your belly. Your shoulders should not go up and down with breathing. It may take a bit of time for you to develop good breathing habits, but stick with it. I know some people who make a point of deep breathing on their daily walk. They count to four as they inhale, hold for another four and then breathe out over four counts. This is a good exercise to practice proper breathing. Increase the number of counts as your lung capacity expands over time.

Step 3: Ground Your Energy and Be Aware of Its Flow

It is important to ground your energy often. Think of your energy as circulating through and around you, connecting you to the universal energy above and below the earth. With each breath, breathe in air and energy from above and around you. When exhaling, imagine forcing that energy down the front of your body, through the soles of your feet to the center of the earth. Feel your soles connecting to the earth's core. The exhale connects you to everything on the planet. The inhale connects you with all in the universe. This is grounding, which is all about being aware of our connection to energy systems. Grounding will increase your physical energy and strength by unifying your aura with other energy systems. It will cleanse your aura and generally improve your health.

Step 4: Drink Water

Drink water. Lots of it. Our bodies are nearly 80 percent water—it composes that much of our body weight. We are water-based creatures, and we must respect this. Every day, drink the eight glasses your body needs. Drink filtered water, if possible. If you want a more exciting taste, add a twist of fresh lime or lemon.

Our bodies need water to operate optimally. If we face an additional health challenge because of an injury or illness, water is a vital part of our recovery. Our bodies remove unwanted and unnecessary materials by excreting them along with the water. This is our natural purification process. Without water, toxins that could easily be removed on a regular basis accumulate in our bodies. Dehydration can be deadly.

Consuming water is the easiest habit to change, and the most overlooked. Water is readily available to most of us and sometimes can alone achieve remarkable results. You would never think of trying to run your car without adding oil and gas. Why would you treat your car with more respect and care than you would your own body? We have been given this fabulously effective body, and it shouldn't be taken for granted.

Step 5: Develop Emotional Bonds with Others

Many of us, but not all, are fortunate enough to have loving family members. And at any moment in time, each and every one of us has the opportunity to bond with others as friends. We all need these emotional connections. It requires a give-and-take of trust to make relationships work, but it is well worth the effort. Welcome it and your world becomes a wonderful, loving place to live, a place filled with good, harmonious energy.

Stable and loving relationships have been shown to have a strong and positive influence on health. Those who have made the effort and commitment to develop close relationships with family members and friends are healthier than those who lack these relationships. If they do get sick or injured, they recover much faster than people who do not have a network of supportive family or friends.

Step 6: Think Positively in the Present Tense and Feel Its Effects

The power of your own positive thoughts helps balance your mental, physical, emotional and spiritual aspects. This balance empowers us, making us able to achieve our dreams and keep us healthy. Stay in the now, as the past is over and, although it is good to have dreams, fears about the future are futile.

Dream of what you truly love to do and do it. Only *you* can make a lasting change in yourself. By looking inward, it is possible to re-create yourself. Be aware of your feelings and your power to adjust and control them.

Put yourself into a quiet meditative state. Picture a three-dimensional holographic image of yourself. This takes lots of concentration and practice. Make it an exact image of yourself. If your eyes are blue, imagine the image of yourself having blue eyes. Visualize it. Concentrate on seeing your eyes exactly as they are. Work on perfecting this image until it is an exact image of you, exact in every detail. Even someone who lacks imagination can do this.

Once you have this clear image in your mind, repeat to yourself that you are all better and problem-free. Concentrate this beam of positive thoughts on the injured area. For example, if you have an elbow problem, project these positive thoughts like a laser beam toward your elbow.

Do not think of the problems. You do not have any problems in the image you have put in front of you. Think of the perfect hologram, one with no injuries. I know this can work for you because of what I do. I heal people with my ability to connect to their energy holograms. Once I connect to a person, I use my thoughts to perform the healing work that I do.

I understand that this ability to connect to a person's hologram is a gift. I also know that we all have the ability to make the connection to our own holograms and use the power of thought to heal. This does not come easily, but with the desire to learn and with some practice, you will succeed. By continuing to practice, you will find that it gets easier and easier, and that your ability to do this increases. Once you master it, you will find this an effective method of improving and maintaining your state of wellness.

Step 7: Understand and Appreciate the Connectedness of Everyone and Everything

Everything affects everything else in the entire universe in a weblike manner. Positive thoughts and actions taken by one of us affect everyone else. While the people most affected are those closest to us in the web—family, friends, workmates and acquaintances—the entire web is indeed affected. It is this interconnectedness that enables distant healing to take place.

Feel grateful for your life—it is precious. Be thankful for all the wonderful people who have connected with you along your journey. Look forward to the adventures that each day brings. We all face challenges, but our attitude as we face them makes all the difference. The positive outlook of each of us is contagious.

In order to get the most out of these seven steps, complete the quiz below. Understanding where you are currently is essential before you can move forward. How do you spend your time? What are your daily routines and your passions? Who do you spend your day with? Self-reflection is essential to understanding yourself. By answering these questions as truthfully as you can, you will be better equipped for your healing journey. Through the self-reflection this quiz will initiate, you will have many insights into yourself. This will help you on your journey as you explore the Seven Steps for Life.

ANALYZE YOUR LIFESTYLE
Habits
Smoking, drinking or recreational drug use: What triggers this habit of yours? Why do you want to smoke, drink or take drugs? What would happen if you quit?

Prescription and nonprescription drugs: Do you know what you are taking and why? Do you know the benefits of the drugs as well as the side effects? Pay attention to the messages your body is sending you.

Diet: Do you maintain a healthy and balanced diet? Try to see yourself as an outsider looking in. If you are overweight in spite of balancing all your food groups, eat smaller portions. A healthy weight results from a balanced equation of input and output: Calories in versus calories burned as fuel for the body's day-to-day functioning. Find your balance. Remember to drink lots of water.

Exercise: Do you have physical activities that you enjoy doing as a part of your daily routine? Do what you are able to and when you are able to. Find an activity you like to do. You will find it easier to integrate any good habit into your lifestyle if it is an enjoyable activity.

Attitudes

Stress: Do you feel weary from the stress of everyday pressures at home and work? Be in control of your stress level, rather than allowing stress to control you. Be aware of how day-to-day stresses affect you: your health, your relationships with others and your view of yourself. Reflect upon this. Eliminate that which affects you negatively.

Positive outlook: Do you see the glass as half empty or half full? Do others close to you radiate with the positive energy that you need?

Flexible: Do you look forward to change and the challenges that it brings? Do you enjoy keeping an open mind toward future possibilities?

If your answer to this question is "No," further self-reflection is needed. Examine why you feel this way. What triggers your resistance to change? Self-reflection is, again, your most useful tool in facing the future with a positive outlook.

Emotions

Useless emotions: Are you worried about your future? Do you feel guilt about some issues? Are you afraid to face some subjects head on? Do you feel angry with someone or something? What triggers these emotions for you? How can you imagine yourself avoiding these trigger situations? You are in control. Get in the driver's seat, learn to identify these hazards and steer clear of them.

Worry, guilt, fear and anger are emotions that serve no purpose, so get rid of them. Examine your reaction to events as they occur in order to understand your resistance to change. Becoming aware of your reaction is the first step to change. Stop yourself from reacting in your usual way and force yourself to react more positively. Just try it and see how it feels. You will consume less energy than if you are fighting change. Let this become your new way of approaching life.

Positive emotions: Do you consciously surround yourself with love and happiness? Love and happiness lead to self-acceptance and acceptance of others. What triggers these emotions for you? Endeavor to create an environment for yourself where these positive triggers figure prominently.

TELEPATHY, INTUITION AND INTENTION IN HEALING

The healing process involves telepathy, intuition and intention. Together, these allow for modifications to be made to the quantum information system of the body.

Telepathy is a form of communication that uses the transfer of images (thought) from one person to another. Once I am connected to a person, I am aware of subconscious and conscious responses of that person. Usually, a person's conscious thoughts dictate their actions, but this is not the case with people in comas. This makes telepathy especially useful in communicating with them. I have had amazing results by sending images to those who can "express" their ideas this way only, because of their infirm state of health. I was once contacted by the family of a man who had had brain surgery and had been in a coma for six months. At a pre-arranged time, I telepathically communicated with him when he was comatose. The energy treatment and telepathic communication immediately awakened him out of this state. After two sessions he was responding to his surroundings and able to see.

Intuition, as I discussed earlier, is another quantum attribute used in the healing process. Intuition is a sense of knowing something without needing to consciously reason about it. Sometimes intuitive information is not easily understood logically, but it usually has something to do with the healing task at hand. You need to learn how to interpret the intuitive data you receive when you are doing self-healing. This information is integrally linked to the healing process.

Intention is one of the most important quantum tools. The intentions of both the healer and the healee are what make things happen. Intention is the driving force that manipulates energy and information systems. When you have a large group of people, all with the same intent to heal someone, their combined intentions produce amazing results. Prayer is one example of an intentional group activity. There have been many studies showing that prayer works. Even if only one individual visualizes his intentions, the results can be amazing.

The intentions of the person being healed must be sincere in order for any significant change to happen. It is not a question of whether people believe in prayer or distant healing. They do not have to believe, but they do need to be open-minded enough to accept that it is possible. It is essential that one intends to get better in order to experience any changes.

Doctors often feel obligated to quote a specific amount of time remaining when confronted with patients they deem terminally ill. This may not be the fault of their training. Patients themselves demand to know. The irony is that many patients are planning their death when they should be planning to regain their health. The mind is powerful, and one's situation is very much controlled by one's beliefs.

There is no such thing as false hope. New directions are always possible. Many people who had been given a death sentence by Western medicine read my first book when it came out. Deep down, they knew I was not able to personally help all of them individually, but they were comforted by the book's message not to give up. They found new hope.

I believe that if we are all connected in life, then we are all connected after we leave our physical bodies. Death is an inevitable event that happens to every living creature. We cannot avoid it. What we can do is improve our health and happiness while we are alive.

Don't get hung up on any one ritual of healing. It is not necessary to jump up and down and click your heels together three times while repeating the phrase "There's no place like home." Healing is simple, and everything you need for healing is within you anywhere and anytime. If it seems like there are too many rules, and it is more complicated than it should be, then you probably have made it so.

Remember that you are always the person in

charge of your own wellness. You are the driver of the car. You make all of the decisions—where you go, when you go there and how fast you travel. The healer is the navigator or map reader, advising you on the easiest route to your destination and assisting as required. Many other people assist—the mechanic who keeps your car safe and the gas station attendant who provides you with fuel. But you are always the driver. You ultimately have total control.

THE EVOLUTION OF SELF-HEALING

The wave of healing knowledge continues to build throughout the Western world. We have a long way to go, but people are beginning to understand and accept that we are all connected to one another and to every living creature in this universe.

We are able to feel empathy with someone who is experiencing sorrow or happiness. The entire world felt the pain of the victims of the 9/11 tragedy. A shiver went through my body when I saw the World Trade towers collapse. I believe that the sensations we felt were a result of our connection to one another. They are like ripples in the sea, which ultimately affects every molecule of water in the vast ocean. Our connection to one another is a vast pool of energy extending in all directions throughout the universe.

It is difficult to grasp the concept of our interconnectedness because of the boundaries we create in our minds. These boundaries are an extension of our limited five senses. If we can't see, smell, feel, hear or taste something, then it most likely doesn't exist—or so we have been taught. In other words, if it can't currently be measured or explained through scientific study, it isn't real. To go beyond these limitations would destabilize the very foundation of our current world view. Our entire physical existence is based on the concept of individual separateness.

Notice that we do accept as real some things not visible to the naked eye. We know that electromagnetic waves are all around us, even though we cannot sense many of their frequencies. Visible light is an electromagnetic frequency that we are able to sense. Radio wave frequencies exist, and they are also in the electromagnetic spectrum, yet we are unable to sense their existence until we tune in to a radio station. The existence of radio waves has been readily accepted for the last hundred years. Accepting our own energy systems will be the next big step. It is just a matter of time before science can measure and understand this phenomenon.

I often get the feeling that I should react to a situation one way, and yet I end up thinking about it and reacting differently. In retrospect, my first reaction was often the better choice. How can I learn to trust my feelings?

We have been taught to undervalue our feelings and place much value on the visible, material world. Society reinforces the idea that if something can't be accurately measured, then it should be ignored. We must relearn not to second-guess our feelings and, indeed, to trust them. As you have said, often our first instinctual reaction to a situation is pure, without rational weighing of alternatives. This may well be the better choice. Practice going with your gut feeling and you will gain more confidence in trusting it. We must forget what we have learned and remember what we have forgotten.

I have been told by my doctor that I have terminal cancer.
How can I think positively about anything now?

How do you envision that thinking negatively will help you? We should all enjoy life while we have it, and now is more important a time than ever for you to be positive. Healing is more than improving the physical self. A true healing encompasses increased wellness and awareness in body, mind and spirit. It's true that death is an inevitable part of life, but nobody can tell you when you will die. It is important to look forward to each and every day, rather than marking the last one in your calendar.

Chapter 5
Group Healing

Your mind holds the wisdom to heal your body.

—ADAM

I receive thousands more requests for individual treatments than I am able to physically do. As I was trying to make sense of being given this healing gift yet having a limited number of hours in a day to use it, I made an incredibly useful discovery: It is possible to merge the auras of two or more people.

Every person's aura looks like a bubble of flowing energy surrounding the physical body. While watching energy demonstrations, I could see the effect that one person's aura had on another. Given that this interaction exists, I wondered whether it was possible to merge several auras.

I had always noticed that in sports the intention

of a movement precedes the actual motion. When a basketball player is thinking about a move in a particular direction, I can see a spike in his aura indicating this intention. Intention is both powerful and visible. What would happen, I wondered, if I combined the intention and interaction of auras? I was eager to find out, so I asked my family to help me with an experiment.

My mom, dad and uncle were willing participants. I asked them to sit fairly close to each other so that their auras were touching. Although their auras still looked separate, they sort of stuck together when touching, just as I had seen happen to auras in a workshop I had attended earlier. Then I asked my parents and uncle to expand their auras by taking in energy from the universe. This allowed their auras to join through intention—like two bubbles in a bath that suddenly burst and form one larger bubble.

THE MASTER HOLOGRAM

Once my parents' and uncle's auras merged, I was able to connect them collectively as one to the universal energy field. (I explain this energy field in more detail in the next chapter.) What I call a master hologram immediately appeared before me. The master hologram contained and combined the information of everyone in the group.

Pleased with the results of this experiment, I was eager to take it a step further. If it was possible to merge auras and manifest a master hologram, could the single master hologram allow information transfers to bring about positive changes to all those present in a larger group?

In the past, I had helped several people with fibromyalgia, a chronic and painful condition with symptoms of muscle tenderness. At present there is no cure for it, so doctors typically prescribe large doses of painkillers to relieve it. How would this master hologram work for a group of people with a similar ailment such as fibromyalgia? I wondered.

It was easy to assemble a group of twelve people with fibromyalgia. Once their auras were merged as one, a master hologram appeared containing all the health information combined. What I discovered was that the master hologram allowed for the transfer of the information to all who were united in a common aura. The information is transferred in the form of energy patterns, of which I am the conduit. By doing the same type of energy transfer treatment that I do for individuals, I was able to convey information to improve the health of all the participants in the group.

This was a wonderful discovery for me and relieved the pressure of having to say no to so many requests because of lack of time and energy. In the fibromyalgia groups, most people noticed immediate and profound improvements in their health. Several participants stated that they no longer even had fibromyalgia. Their painful symptoms are gone.

These results opened the door to continued group treatments, but I wanted to be sure I was on the right track. I emailed *Apollo 14* astronaut Edgar Mitchell, one of my physics mentors, for his opinion and feedback on this breakthrough. This is his reply:

"Very interesting comments and effects. Regarding how it fits into the QH [quantum hologram] theory: Although each individual has a separate and distinct holographic record, you seem to have helped them resonate with each other and with you as a group, almost like an athletic team that is 'in the zone' and functioning as one. If they all have the same disease, then that disease has a distinct holographic pattern. Presumably, healing involves an inverse wave (or set of waves) to the pattern of the disease. It is interesting that you could have an effect on all just by focusing on the disease pattern. But, theoretically, no reason why not."

Edgar has been an invaluable source of information throughout the development of my healing abilities and I always appreciate his input. His scientific explanations ring true to me.

LESSONS FROM NATIVE CULTURE

Several hundred years ago, the Europeans conquered a medically advanced civilization in North America, that of the Native people. In Native cultures, people know how to use nature to heal the body. Many alternative healing methods ceased when these cultures were suppressed. The type of medicine that was practiced so effectively for thousands of years was outlawed.

My dad has Native American family on his mother's side. They belong to the Penobscot Indian Nation, based in the state of Maine. I have always been proud of my Native heritage and its connection with nature and the universal energy.

Native people accept the reality of spirit and energy interconnectedness. This makes them a pleasure to work with. The Cree language has one word, "mamaweska," to express a concept that takes seven words to express in English: "Our universal connection to everyone and everything." Visualizations and dreams are an integral part of Native cultures and have great meaning. We would do well to learn this connection to our inner power from our Native neighbors. Native people understand that energy is in and around everything. They are aware that it connects and influences everything. This connection with nature and its universal energy is regarded with the utmost respect.

It was shortly after I began my work in group healing that I was invited to be one of the ten healers at the Nekaneet First Nations International Healing Gathering to be held in Saskatchewan during the summer of 2003. The Nekaneet people, who are part of the Cree Nation, hosted the event. What an honor it was to be there.

Soon after our family's arrival, we were taken to the windswept grasslands where the Nekaneet people have lived for many centuries. Ten teepees were set up in a healing circle, with a fire pit in the center. I was given a choice of teepees to conduct my healings in. We had arrived fairly early, so only one had already been selected. It didn't take me long to choose one that backed onto a thick grove of trees. A constant breeze picked up the sweet scent of grass.

Then we quickly joined the others as they headed up the path to watch the youth riders approach on horseback. A horse and rider could be seen in the distance between the rolling hills. Soon there were more than twelve, all riding toward us. It was a magical sight, surely reminiscent of centuries past.

An eagle staff was held high by the leader of the procession. The riders were greeted by the elders, who, by teaching their knowledge, are the link between the past and the future. A ceremony to honor the riders commenced. It was an awesome scene. The next morning, the gathering opened with the traditional healing dance around the fire, accompanied by singing and drumming. Then I started a day of healing in my teepee.

The Nekaneet people and others who attended the Gathering understood that the balancing of mind, body and spirit is what a healing journey is about. They were aware that spirit is the intuitive part of self. As well, there was an overwhelming sense that being in such a beautiful setting was therapeutic in and of itself; it was the perfect spot for reflection. I also had the honor of working with several shaman and learned to understand more about their traditional ways.

Native elders and organizers demonstrated the incredible dedication and enormous effort that has kept their culture and way of life alive. I will never forget the powerful energy and emotion I felt at this Gathering. The traditional healers were committed to helping anyone who needed healing. They spent long hours in the hot sun helping all who showed up, sharing their knowledge and healing skills.

With hundreds of people waiting in line for treatment, I felt it was best to try group treatments. Before this, the only group healings I had done was of people with similar ailments. Nevertheless, I proceeded with varied groups. My teepee held twelve people comfortably, so I treated four groups of twelve per day, in addition to a few individual healings. Everyone, either through their culture or their personal interest, understood the basis of energy healing, which made my introduction of the topic easy. The group treatments were very successful. One woman left my teepee after a session without needing her cane to walk. My dad found the cane and ran out of the teepee to give it to her, calling out, "I guess you don't need this anymore." Everyone had a good laugh.

By the last day of the Gathering I had a waiting list of over three hundred, so I decided to try something different. I asked permission of the elders to use the big open-air tent for a large group healing.

They agreed, and it was announced over the PA system. Hundreds of people showed up.

I looked at the crowd that filled the tent and quickly realized that, although most of the people were familiar with energy treatments, many would be unfamiliar with the concept of grounding their energy, and that a group healing would not be manageable. So, instead, I asked that only the first two rows participate in the healing. This amounted to about eighty-five people. Everyone else had to move well back in order not to interfere with the energy of the participating group.

The results were fascinating—to me and to everyone else. We all felt that a powerful healing connection had been made. I heard numerous stories of changes in health-related issues when I spoke with the group after the treatment. Pain issues and breathing problems had the most immediate positive changes. I heard later from people with other health issues that their problems had also improved.

It was interesting that the visions people received during the healing had a common theme, which seemed to flow from person to person. A man in the center said that he saw vividly an eagle soaring with outstretched wings and wind in its feathers. Others on either side of him also saw feathers and felt wind on their backs. This vision gradually changed to a strong wind blowing from behind. It was incredible how people connected to one another in this state. Many were in tears, overwhelmed by the energy in the tent. This was a fabulous learning experience for me. Out of necessity, I had discovered that many people could take part in a collective treatment.

GROUP HEALING WORKSHOPS

Since I have come to the realization that group treatments are possible, I have held numerous group workshops across North America. My intention is to help as many people as I possibly can. In the process, I am continually learning more about my abilities.

The main point that I emphasize in these workshops is that everyone does have the ability to improve their own health. Specifically, I do these workshops to help people manage their own health issues, not to solve their problems for them. The group aspect of treatment provides a strong energy connection that enhances your own healing ability. After you experience this connection, healing yourself becomes easier. There is nothing that impacts our memory like experience itself. Feeling this connection is more powerful than any academic knowledge of it. This is what people take away with them from the workshops.

In the workshops I explain what I do as simply as possible and report the movement of energy exactly as I see it. I provide both the scientific explanations and the simple analogies of the healing phenomenon, which allows everyone to acquire a general understanding of the healing process.

Just as my abilities are evolving, so are the workshops. My first workshop had only twelve participants. The number at each has gradually increased to several hundred. The combined and focused energy of these group sessions is powerful. I still get many requests for individual treatments, and continually remind people not to underestimate the power of group treatments.

The workshops have proven to be an excellent step toward wellness for many people. Currently, each workshop consists of two group treatments, from which everyone can benefit, whether they have an immediate health concern or not. For people who are very sensitive to subtle energy, one group treatment may be all they need to return to their state of wellness. During these group sessions, attendees experience what it feels like to connect to infinite healing energy, for which I act as a conduit.

Once people feel this connection, they are able to return to it more readily and easily on their own to continue with their self-healing. It is like riding a bike. Once we master what seems an impossible balancing act, we gain an unforgettable lifelong skill.

STEPS IN GROUP HEALING

At the outset of a workshop, I teach the participants to, first, ground their energy to expand their auras and, second, join their auras with those around them. Although grounding is always helpful, it is only necessary to join auras for a group healing.

Illustration 9:
Grounding your energy:
Visualize tree roots branching out from your feet

Illustration 10: *Grounding your energy:*
Pulling the energy of the entire universe into you

Illustration 11: *Grounding your energy:* Your expanded aura

Step I: Ground Your Energy to Expand Your Aura

1. Visualize tree roots branching out from your feet. These roots branch out to more roots until the entire energy of the earth is engulfed in your roots (see Illustration 9).

2. On inhalation, pull the earth's infinite energy into you. Once you are supersaturated with this energy, your aura will expand naturally, since merely having this intention will make it happen.

3. On exhalation, push the energy now in your head down your body and out your feet, connecting with the earth.

Another method of grounding is to imagine that you are in a vacuum. On inhalation, feel the energy of the entire universe being pulled into you (see Illustration 10). This will cause your aura to enlarge.

It does not matter which visualization you do as long as your intentions are to ground and expand your aura. Illustration 11 shows what your expanded aura might look like. (When auras are

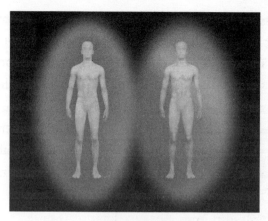

Illustration 12a:
*Joining your aura
to those around you:* Auras sticking

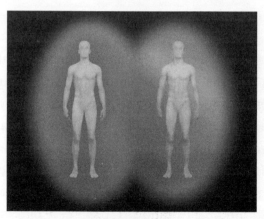

Illustration 12b:
Joining your aura to those around you:
Auras merging

merged, they appear white or grayish as the group reaches an overall common frequency.)

Energy is easily influenced by intention. With the simple intention of taking in excess energy, one does exactly that: take in energy. Once you have become supersaturated with this energy, the only place that energy can go is out. As a result, the aura expands.

Step 2: Join Your Aura to That of Those Around You

When the aura is in an expanded state, it has the temporary ability to merge with other auras in the same expanded state. Now the group can join their auras as one.

Once you have allowed your aura to expand, shift your visualizing focus to connecting the auras. Visualize your aura merging with the auras of those around you—just as two bubbles in a bath merge into one larger bubble—until there are no divisions between persons. Illustrations 12 (a and b) and 13 show this process. A bird's-eye view of the room would be of one large aura that

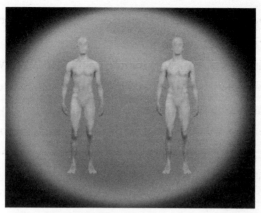

Illustration 13:
Joining your aura to those around you:
Auras joined as one

Illustration 14:
Energy at a group treatment

fills the room. When people are close together, their auras stick. They don't totally connect, but they adhere somewhat. If the participants' energy is grounded and super-energized, this adherence is more pronounced.

Step 3: The Master Hologram

Now the group is merged as one. This is the same oneness that is evident on a smaller scale within each of us. Your body is composed of trillions of cells, and every cell has its own distinct aura. On a larger scale, these cells are all resonating harmoniously together to form your own complete and uniform aura. Just as the auras of each cell within us connects and works together for our own benefit, each of our auras can be connected to benefit all within the group.

What appears before me is a master hologram—an image of a body with a collection of all the problems of the group. A change to the master hologram affects everyone in the group. With a group of several hundred people with various health issues, there is no way I can focus on every detail in the master hologram. What I can do is send as much energy through it as possible and, for many people, that is all that is needed for their problem to be corrected. It's difficult to portray what I see energetically and work with during a group treatment, but Illustration 14 will give you a general idea.

When the master hologram appears before me, there is an intelligent communication of energy information. This enables me to receive and deliver healing information to where it is needed. For example, if I receive and send information about adjustments needed for a person's back pain, only those who need back healing information receive it. In each group, I address as many areas of the body as I can during the twenty-minute or so session. (And, as I mentioned earlier, group healings are even more effective when everyone in the group has one common illness. When I adjust the master hologram for that specific illness, everyone in the group benefits more directly.)

At the same time that I am working with the master hologram, the group members are doing their individual visualizations in the manner that

I've outlined to them. Everyone seems to know somehow where they need to send healing energy. Each person knows best what she personally needs. This is not necessarily a conscious thought, although people often come to the workshops concerned about a particular problem. I tell participants to just let the energy move naturally to wherever it is needed in the body, since energy healing is a natural process. Positive intentions will bring only positive results.

My experience during a group treatment is similar to that of an individual treatment. During any treatment, everything in the room goes dark and then I see a three-dimensional image, or hologram, in front of me. Next, the information appears before me in a format resembling a holographic computer screen. I can access the information in layers or subsets. I zoom in or out depending on what is needed to get the clearest and most helpful view. Then, with the energy of my focused intention, I can add or delete things to the hologram to initiate change. All the information is in a form that I can manipulate with my intentions.

What I am physically doing at this point is moving my arms, hands and fingers around. I became aware of this only after my parents told me that I do this and my dad filmed me. This movement makes sense to me: Verbal communication—body language—is often used to enhance what we are saying.

During an individual treatment, I connect to the person by allowing myself to resonate at her frequency. In a group treatment, once the auras of all the participants have merged as one, I choose a person at random and connect to her, just as I would during an individual treatment. For a moment I see only that person's hologram. An instant later, I see the image branch out to include everyone in the group; that is, a master hologram emerges, which I then work with.

Everyone has a role to play in this participatory group healing experience. I act as the conduit for the energy and as a facilitator by organizing and directing the energy to where it is needed. My primary role is to assist people in reaching the optimum resonance for accessing their health information. From this point, their own life energy takes over, and the information becomes intelligible to them. In this manner, I help people remember what they have forgotten. They become empowered to make positive changes in order to help themselves. The instruction to heal comes from you—your intentions—since your mind has the wisdom to heal your body.

If everyone joins auras, will I pick up any bad energy from others in the group?
I'm inevitably asked this question at every workshop. No, it doesn't work that way. There is no negative energy. There is no positive energy either. The energy is simply that which is directed through our intentions. It makes no sense to attach attributes such as "good" or "bad" to energy, as it reacts and moves according to your intentions. Keep every intention focused on healing and only positive results can occur.

Is a group treatment of fifty people more effective than one with five hundred attendees?

I am often asked this question, as many people think that the energy will be divided between all participants. This is not so. A healing workshop is filled with positive healing intentions. The more positive energy, the more everyone in the room can feel its intensity and effects. It truly seems to be a case of "the more the merrier."

Many studies have been conducted on the positive effects that a group of focused people can have as they create a collective consciousness. This common intention resonates throughout our interconnectivity to influence events far beyond ourselves.

Visualizations are focused intention. The workshops allow all participants to feel the power of energy and learn to direct it within themselves.

Why do you think that doing visualizations can positively influence oneself?

I know that visualizations can work because I can see the energy flow. When a person is directing his focused healing intentions through visualizations, I see the flow of energy interacting within him. A balanced and harmonious-looking flow returns as the body energy shifts to influence that person's wellness.

Chapter 6

The Physics of Energy Healing

Ill health is an imbalance of energy.

—ADAM

MATTER AS ENERGY

Einstein's most famous formula, $E=mc^2$, states that when you annihilate matter, you will get a certain amount of energy as a result. This means that matter is simply compressed energy and therefore everything in the universe is energy. When you throw a stone into a pond, every molecule in the pond is affected as a result of the ripple. Similarly, thoughts and intentions are a form of energy that radiate from you, affecting everything in the sea of energy—the universe.

As we zoom our focus in on matter with a microscope, it starts to look like Swiss cheese. The more we zoom in, the more we are able to see the increase in space within what formerly appeared to be solid matter. As magnification increases, solidity increasingly disappears and space expands. If we did find solid matter, it would be of infinite density, and that is impossible. There is no such thing as solid matter. The more you break things down, the more you find that everything is just vibrations. The bottom line is that everything and everyone is energy.

Once we realize that our bodies are all energy, we can appreciate the interconnectedness we have between every cell within us and between every living organism in the universe. Our thoughts, emotions and mental and physical energies emit outward in all directions. They affect others around and close to us in positive and negative ways.

Quantum string theory states that matter is energy, which is a frequency or a vibration. Everything in the universe is made up of energies that vibrate at different frequencies and in different patterns.

Ill health is an imbalance of energy. Energy

imbalance manifests itself in the form of different ailments, depending on where we develop an energy blockage. Energy blockages, frequently first experienced as stress, manifest differently from person to person. Some people are more prone to headaches, for example, and others to stomach aches when under stress. A communication breakdown occurs when our energy systems are not flowing in a harmonious pattern. What I refer to as our pattern of wellness is the result of our energy systems flowing in a harmonious pattern.

The goal of every cell is to communicate in harmony with every other cell. On a larger scale, it can be extrapolated that every living being wants to be in harmony and communicate effectively with every other being.

The science behind a group treatment is the merging of these energy systems, the auras, into one large, vibrating energy system. My part is tuning the group to a coherent frequency that makes this merging possible—like an orchestra conductor. Then everyone in the group is resonating at the same frequency, commonly referred to as "getting in tune."

As a coherent energy pattern emerges, people feel this synergistic effect of resonating at the same frequency. Healing occurs when an energetic change or, more accurately, an information adjustment to one person in the group causes that identical change to everyone in the group. I act as a conduit, connecting the group to this energetic change. During a group healing, all the individual auras are connected with no divisions between individual auras.

Nature shows us examples of vibrating energies merging into one. Have you ever noticed that when a flock of birds is disturbed on the ground, they all fly away at the same time? Similarly, when you frighten a school of fish, they all turn away simultaneously, as though connected to a common grid, and swim in the same direction. Every particle in their bodies is connected to every other particle. The impulse to move, originating in one fish, radiates outward in all directions instantaneously. An inaudible alarm bell has rung out a simple message to all.

Another force of nature not to be overlooked is water. One drop is relatively powerless as a moving force, but lots of drops flowing together have reshaped our planet many times over. That's how group treatments work. The thoughts or intentions of many form the energy force that attracts and empowers the collective reality.

THE UNIVERSAL ENERGY FIELD

We all tune in to our various senses by picking up various energy frequencies. Our sensory system works like a radio tuner. Imagine the dial on a radio having words on it that trigger memories instead of numbers for stations. As you turn the dial, you tune in to what you recall of that memory, including sights, smells, sounds, tastes and feelings. Everything we pick up with our sensory tuner is information from the universal energy field (UEF). Everything that ever existed registers as information recorded in this field.

Every bit of information we hold in our minds is from the universal energy field. We all differ in our capacities to tap into this information. That is part of what makes us unique. Memory is the process of neurons in the brain forming and remembering patterns that help us connect to specific parts of the field.

To elaborate, when we have different thoughts, all we are doing is pulling the information out of the UEF. Our minds then organize, process and interpret this information so that it has local meaning—that is, so that it becomes meaningful to us in our physical reality. Of course, some people are more adept than others at accessing this information, just as some people are more naturally athletic than others.

Not all information is perceived by our five senses. It is much more efficient to bypass this sensory level and go straight to just knowing. It is a little like cracking an egg: You don't need to crack an egg to know what is inside; you just know from experience and trust in this. The brain's natural tendency is to process information in the most efficient way possible. Because of the interconnection we have with everything, the brain can use its quantum processing ability to interpret information with maximum efficiency.

OUR ENERGY LINKS

Living organisms share a common energy that links them together. The energy that connects us behaves in various ways at various frequency or vibrational patterns. As I mentioned earlier, it is for this reason that it is inaccurate to give attributes such as "good" or "bad" to universal energy. No matter which vibrational energy pattern is operating in one's body, it is not transferable to another person's body unless both intend for it to be transferred.

If two or more people meditate together or join auras in a group treatment, their brain wave patterns become synchronized to the most orderly and coherent energy pattern in the group. This can be compared to the body's cells working in unison to form the body's aura.

DISTANT HEALING

Many people tend to think of distant healing as the waving of a magic wand. That is not the case. First, participation from both the healer and healee is required. The healer doesn't directly do the healing but simply directs the healee's immune system to the problem.

The science or the mechanism of the healer's contact is still not fully understood within quantum physics. Space and time—that is, moving from point A to point B—has no meaning in the quantum world of energy connection. So, the healing connections do not travel so much as register instantaneously according to processes that we don't yet fully understand. What we do know is that the positive intentions of both people operate outside conventional notions of time and space. There are no limits to what can be achieved by accessing the quantum realm.

Many physicists now state that barriers separating us from each other are illusions. Understanding this is a step toward accepting that we are all connected. Then we will begin to see ourselves as part of an energy system that is connected to the entire universe.

I have heard of people connecting to "bad" energy. What would you tell them?

Do not think in terms of "good" or "bad" energy—that is, do not think about energy in any emotionally charged sense. It is just energy and is neither good nor bad. The intention is the driving force behind it.

Chapter 7
Skills for Self-Healing Visualizations

Trust yourself and your positive intentions.

—ADAM

Visualizations are concentrated or focused intentions in the form of mental images. A visualization directs your immune system to the problem and guides its action. Visualizations should mirror reality as closely as possible in order to more accurately direct the immune system.

Strong visualization skills will provide you with a solid foundation for self-empowerment. You can enhance these skills by practicing specific strategies such as fine-tuning your ability to visualize, projecting a hologram and recalling details. Be sure also to address general improvements in your lifestyle and attitudes, as discussed in Chapter 4.

FINE-TUNING YOUR ABILITY
TO VISUALIZE

One of the most important requirements for healing is being able to fine-tune the ability to visualize—to see vivid images in your mind's eye. An intention regarding a cut would be simply for it to get better. A visualization can and should be much more specific. For example, visualize the entire healing process taking place in your mind, step by step. First, see the blood platelets clot around the wound. Then imagine the entire healing process taking place, until there is no doubt in your mind that it is complete and that you are healed.

The most effective way to come up with suitable visualizations is to fully understand your problem that needs healing. Do research and learn as much about the illness and the anatomy of the injured area as you can. Because the mind is integrally linked to the immune system, having the visualizations as anatomically correct as possible will more accurately direct the immune system toward the specific problem. Know what white blood cells look like so that when you visualize them attacking the problem in their attempt to heal, your visual image of them is accurate. This will help you guide your healing intentions more precisely to the source of the problem. Also explore the mental or emotional aspects of the issue. It is important to make use of every tool available to you on your healing journey.

The better you are at visualizing, the easier it will be for you to heal yourself and others. When you are visualizing, it is important to know that it is going to work. In other words, if you convince yourself that your body is being healed, you will act on that belief by healing yourself.

Create a visualization. Continue practicing this visualization until you dream about it. Your body heals best when you are asleep or in a subconscious state. When you dream your visualizations, your body will naturally heal itself. In your dream state, you cannot distinguish between the visualization and reality; therefore, your visualization can become your reality.

Breathe energy into every cell. Every cell has a survival instinct; with this life purpose, cells communicate with other cells, passing on information about any changes within their immediate environment. The soul or total energetic body binds all cells into one functioning harmonious pattern of energy.

When using any visualization, remember to envision your healthy body. Your harmonious immune system is balanced and strong and you are resonating with it positively and confidently. Remember that your visualizations are limited not by the boundaries of your five senses but by your imagination—which is limitless.

PROJECTING A HOLOGRAM

An important skill for healing others and also in maintaining your own health is the ability to project a mental image or a hologram in front of you. When you use energy to heal someone, you must be able to mentally visualize that person. If you are planning to heal yourself, you can rely more heavily on feel, as you can do the visualizations directly on your body. You can also project your own image in front of you, or do both once you are comfortable with this concept. With practice, this becomes more natural. If you are not yet seeing this projection of yourself clearly, relax. With the constant intention of seeing this visualization, you will.

A hologram is a three-dimensional projection that contains all the information—past, present and future—of the person, place or thing to which it belongs. A person's optimum state of wellness is within his hologram. It is this specific information that differentiates a hologram from a simple image. (The two are not interchangeable, although for instructional purposes, I use the word "image" if it is most easily understood within the context.) Of course, it is important to understand this difference when doing healing on another person.

When healing others at a distance, it is necessary to project an image in front of you. As a guideline, this image can be the person's full body form projected in a two-foot-tall hologram. The size of the hologram is not crucial, as long as you can see the full body in your mind's eye. (I see holograms as an actual three-dimensional object, but for many people who are just beginning to learn to heal, it may be easier to think in terms of

doing a visualization.) You will then see the modifications needed on this image.

Many people find it helpful to have a photograph
of the person they are working with, even if it is
someone they know well. Start with this simple two-
dimensional image as a base for your visualizations.
With practice and intuition, this data base will
expand with intelligent information. Eventually, you
will get to a comfort zone where a connection to
the person's quantum information, or quantum
hologram, appears.

Trust yourself and your positive intentions.
Intentions and thoughts are natural forces of nature,
just as gravity is. Once you are able to visualize a
person's holographic image in front of you, the next
step is to use your intention (along with their participatory intentions) to assist them with their
healing.

Concentrate on the injured area. Visualize the
problem being resolved in the hologram. At that
moment it is literally being adjusted in the person's
physical body. Know that this is happening.

Use your hands and arms to manipulate the

thoughts and energies as you see best. Be sure that after you remove the energy blockages or unhealthy cells, you dispose of them into space. Remember that energy is dispersed according to your intentions. Create your own visualization of throwing unwanted material into a vacuum, the garbage or a black hole. Without a host organism, it will dissipate instantly.

RECALLING DETAILS

Have you ever thought about how you think? Think about it: How do you think? Do you think in images? Do you think in terms of your own voice narrating events and thoughts throughout the day? Would the transition from one thought to another make sense to anybody but yourself? How would someone follow the common thread between your thoughts? Spend a moment reflecting on this. It is important to be aware of how we process thoughts in order to be able to change them where necessary.

Telepathy is communicating through pictures or images, which convey richer and more detailed information than any words used to express that thought. A picture is worth a thousand words, they say. I refer to speech as "crude acoustical communication," as there is so much room for misinterpretation of words. We have all experienced such misunderstandings.

Telepathy is easier to have with animals than with people because the transition from one image to another is simpler. My cat, for example, appears to have only about three images: food, sleep, litter box. That's pretty straightforward.

How vivid are the images you create in your mind? In order to visualize more effectively, practice thinking in detailed images. Try staring at an image for thirty seconds; really burn it into your mind's eye. Would someone looking at your mental image right now be able to tell what it is? Most people find it very difficult to create vivid images in their minds.

To improve your visualization skills, learn to think in graphic images rather than in words. Changing our habits from thinking in words to thinking in images takes practice. It is like any other physical training we do: Practice makes perfect.

You will need to be disciplined in your mental training. People who have a photographic memory will most likely have an easier time, but anyone can train himself to remember more visual details. Concentrate on every little detail about a person. Remember her eye color, wrinkles, scars, nose shape, hairstyle, height, weight, physique, and so on. The more you practice this, the more natural and habitual it will become.

To help train yourself to remember more visual details, practice by looking at pictures of people and then trying to fix images of their faces in your mind. To form an image of yourself in your mind, stand in front of a mirror, then close your eyes and recall what you look like.

An easy beginning exercise is to visualize people you know when you are talking to them on the phone. Each time you speak to them, picture them in greater detail. Build an image of them in your mind's eye. Make it a habit. You will find that it gets easier with practice. This will prove to you that you can increase your capacity to recall details and visualize.

A woman approached me after a workshop saying that she couldn't visualize. I asked her if she was planning to attend my workshop the next day, to which she responded, "Yes."

"Do you know where it will be held?" I asked her. "Right here in the same room, isn't it?" she replied.

"Yes. So how will you find it?" I asked. "Will you need to ask anyone how to find the room, or will you rely on images stored in your memory of where you were today to find this same room tomorrow?"

That is when she realized that she does in fact visualize habitually. Visual information is stored solely in nonverbal images—there's no remembering a specific label or room number. This woman will know that the room is through the lobby and to the right. She will have an image in her mind as to the approximate size and shape of the room, so it will look familiar to her the next time she sees it. By becoming more aware of her natural visualizing ability and through practice, she can improve on something she does all the time.

We would be considered dysfunctional if we were unable to recall simple images without too much trouble. Everyone visualizes constantly; we just don't recognize this process for what it is.

Practice taking photographs in your mind's eye of people, places and events. Think in terms of being able to tell a story to someone using those images that you have "photographed." Every time you practice this, the story becomes clearer to the outside observer. More importantly, it also becomes much clearer to you. Imagine someone grating his fingernails on a chalkboard. I bet you have shivers up and down your spine from just the thought of it.

See yourself living your own personal shocking event, such as skydiving if you are afraid of heights. Feel the fear.

Imagine that you are in a tropical paradise. See the sun shimmering on the horizon; hear the waves crashing; feel the soft sand on your bare feet; smell the salt air in the breeze; taste the cold coconut drink on your lips. When you get proficient at this, your body does not know whether this actually occurred in physical reality or only in your imagination. In other words, eventually your body responds to your mental images as if they were physically real. That is the true power of visualization.

FOUR STRATEGIES FOR ENHANCING YOUR VISUALIZATION SKILLS

The next four strategies for enhancing your visualization skills are important reminders of issues I raised earlier about changes in your life. Implementing these suggestions will not only increase your powers of visualization but provide a foundation for self-empowerment. Remember that visualization and self-empowerment skills go beyond the visual connection. We must feel that we are intimately connected to ourselves and are at one with our goal of wellness.

I. Know Yourself

By guiding your emotions, intuition and memories of events (both past, present and future), you are fine-tuning your immune system to heal your body. Your mind has control over every bodily function, so use every tool you have to make all your body systems work for you in the best possible way.

Rather than reacting to emotional triggers with habitual responses, you will become proactive in the creation of new healthier thoughts and reactions. You will be choosing to take in only information that you need to improve your well-being.

Know that you can go beyond any limitations that you may have previously felt based on input from others. Reach confidently toward a new set of expectations of self-empowerment. Understand that you are responsible for yourself.

To understand yourself better, notice what pushes your buttons. What are your emotional triggers? When you understand this, you can control and then reinvent yourself. When we are in control of our conscious and subconscious selves, we are in control of our immune system and our health.

In your dream state (when meditating or about to fall asleep), synchronize your conscious and subconscious mind through visualization. Let your intentions and intuitions guide you. Trust yourself.

2. Improve Your Lifestyle

Get rid of any obvious poor lifestyle habits, including those that cause you stress and bring negativity to your life. The physical part of doing might prove to be the easiest: Work less and play more. Spend time with family and friends. While work is obviously still important, everyone needs to have fun and time to relax. Everyone needs nurturing human ties.

3. Balance Your Life

A basic principle of wellness is achieving balance in all aspects of life: physically, emotionally and spiritually. This is especially important for those who see their role in life as primarily one of helping. However, "giving all" by helping others can become a highly stressful burden when, in the process, you forget to take care of yourself. This can be a pitfall for a healer or caregiver, as the parable of the alcoholic-turned-healer I told earlier in the book illustrates. Achieving balance is everyone's constant challenge, not just the healer's. When imbalance occurs in any area of our lives, it always teaches us about ourselves.

Balance and counterbalance is the ever-changing

dance of life. There aren't any specific guidelines for this, since our challenges are individual. Dance lessons can teach you basic steps, but ultimately it is enjoying the music, developing self-confidence and letting go of inhibitions that enable you to just do it.

4. Be Positive

Surround yourself with positive, like-minded people. Concentrate on what you enjoy. With circumstances you cannot change, learn to change your attitude. Find an aspect about the situation for which you can be grateful and dwell on that.

Monitor self-talk to ensure that what you are telling yourself is positive and reflects your personal goal of wellness. Your expected outcome must be synchronized with your goal: Be sure that you really expect your goal to manifest.

The following five steps will help you to become a more positive person.

Step 1: Eliminate Negative Feedback

Weed out all the negative feedback from your own self-talk and from those around you, and replace it with whatever you need to in order create your new, positive reality. Remember that self-talk is 24–7. This makes you the most influential person in your life. Monitor what you say to yourself about yourself. Once you become aware of this and the influence it has, you will be surprised at how easy it is to consciously dismiss your own subconscious views and attitudes. Change all the self-talk to positive encouragement. Be proud of the changes that you have made.

Step 2: Resist Self-Judgment

All day and all night, we listen to our own judgmental opinions of ourselves. Retire from the exhausting position of being your own judge and jury. Relax and step back as if you were an outside observer. We tend to be hardest on ourselves, so practice self-acceptance. Be your own guide through your best intentions. Approve of yourself through your new eyes.

Step 3: Resist Judgment of Others

Give others—and ultimately yourself—the benefit of the doubt and then move on. How could we possibly expect to judge another's thoughts, words and actions when it is often difficult to assess our own? It is not easy to forgive and forget, but the person holding onto the grudge does harm to herself. When you do this, you are letting an issue in the past grind away at you continuously. Forgive those around you, and with that you will forgive yourself and be free to grow. Forgive, and then forget. Relax and go with it. You will ultimately achieve what you desire.

Step 4: Leave Past Issues in the Past

Leave your personal baggage of anger and fear behind you and move forward. Whatever happened in your past has already happened. It can't be changed. Accept it, move past it. You can't change that the event occurred, but you can change your attitude toward it.

Step 5. Keep It Simple

In our society, we consider it necessary to consult an expert on almost every aspect of our lives. When faced with baffling calculations, we must see an accountant. We ask a lawyer to explain the meaning of a string of indecipherable words. When our body is sending us a personal SOS, we consult a doctor. Many of us have the idea that whatever the situation, it must be complicated. Healing through your own intentions to return to wellness is simple.

Energy constantly flows within each and every one of us. We just need to provide it with some direction. There is no right or wrong way to do visualizations. My suggestions are simply meant to help you to focus more efficiently. Whatever works for you is the right way. It is an individual choice. Through intention, your wish is your command. This will become your reality. Your intentions or thoughts create your own reality. It sounds too simple to be true, but it is.

In the next chapter, I explain some general visualizations that you can use until your own creative juices kick in. Then you will have the feel of it and the confidence to customize your visualizations. Most important is your intention to return to wellness and your knowing that it is possible.

The general pattern to wellness is a healthy lifestyle reinforced by positive attitudes and specific visualization techniques. Remember the transition of the following statements as they apply to your wellness. This three-point belief system should help you reinforce your primary objective:

1. You think that you can be well again.
2. You know that you will return to a healthy state.
3. You are well again.

Visualize yourself in your optimum state of wellness. How are you feeling? What are you doing, thinking and saying? Imagine yourself being well and enjoy it.

I have difficulty visualizing. What do you recommend?
Visualizing is something that we all inherently do, but many of us are unaware of this. So the first step is to be more aware of your ability to do it. Take a mental photograph of the cover of this book as you hold it in your hands. Close your eyes and visualize

it in your mind's eye as you recall the image, colors and any other details. Repeat the process again and increase the amount of detail that you are focusing on. With this intention in mind, you will expand your capacity to effectively visualize. Change the colors of what you see while holding your focus. Remember this process of challenging yourself until it becomes second nature.

How long should I visualize for?
There is no set time for the length of a visualization; it varies from person to person. Some people can visualize for hours while others can only do it for a few minutes. If you lose your focus and want to continue with your visualizations, just relax, refocus and start over. Do not push yourself. The idea is not to log a lot of time but to make the visualizations as real as possible.

Chapter 8

General Visualizations: Re-creating Wellness

Visualizations are tools to empower you.

—ADAM

Visualization is more than using our sense of sight alone. We should be achieving a realistic feeling of actually experiencing the event. That is when we know that we are doing it right. Mastering visualization will give you the confidence that you need for self-empowerment. These are resources that we all have at our fingertips; we just have to tap into them.

Think of your new ideal self as your goal. Then learn that you can and you will achieve this goal. Your body has everything it needs to heal itself. Think of all your reasons to stay well and visualize them happening with you. Setting this goal and visualizing it will lead to your success.

There is a constant exchange of information between your quantum hologram and your physical body. Visualizations are tools to empower you to take control of this information exchange process. This is how you can direct your immune system to the desired location to maximize health benefits. It's that simple.

When you have a chronic problem, your body becomes so accustomed to it that it compensates for it. To put it another way, the body overlooks and ignores the problem; essentially, it no longer knows about the problem. And so, your immune system doesn't do anything about it.

Visualizations show your body that there is a problem. Your doing visualizations demonstrates to yourself that you are serious about making a change. Maintain the constant intention to make the visualizations work.

Visualizing involves integration and flow of your thoughts. It is very important to synchronize your conscious and subconscious intentions, since the more harmonious the intentions are, the more effective they tend to be. This means that the level of consciousness you're at when you can say out loud, "I know I can do it" is in harmony with that little subconscious voice deep inside you. Your outcome expectation must also be in harmonious agreement with your visualization and intention.

General visualizations are dramatic interpretations of how we are going to re-create our wellness. What these lack in specifics they make up for in dramatic impressions. Put as much realistic sight, sound and feeling as you can into each visualization, while holding your positive intentions and ultimate goal in mind. Strive to achieve a realistic feeling of actually experiencing the event. When you do have this feeling, you will have fully mastered the technique.

The following universal or general visualizations will benefit you regardless of the injury or illness. You may visualize these images directly on your physical self, or you may project these on a hologram in front of you, or both. These may also be done to a hologram of someone else, but not at the same time as you are working on yourself, as the energy gets dispersed, diminishing the effect. You can do the visualizations sitting, standing or lying down; just make sure that you are comfortable when doing them.

These are the stages for self-healing using visualizations:

1. Form the image (eventually the hologram) of yourself, or of the person you are healing, as described in Chapter 7.
2. Focus on your goal by using visualizations to:
   a. Exit your existing pattern of injury or illness.
   b. Reboot your system through intense visualizations (this will occur automatically).
   c. Reset your system to what is desired.
   d. Set your pattern of wellness in place.

You may find it helpful to practice saying the visualization steps out loud. The mere intention of visualizing will make it happen. Don't just say you will try: Do it.

There are five universal visualizations I recommend: Fire and ice temperature extremes, Lightning bolts, Smart Energy Packets, Explosion and Waterfall. The first four, including your personal adaptations, can be done in any order. Try them all and see which works best for you. Do all of them at various times, and you might find that a particular order works well. Use the waterfall visualization last in the sequence of visualizations you decide upon. This visualization calms, relaxes and cleanses your system: You have visualized the removal of your problem; now you must repattern or reprogram yourself.

Visualizations help maintain our healthy state as well. No matter what the health challenge was, you should continue to routinely practice your visualizations. They will ensure that your energy flows harmoniously without blockages long after your physical ailment has been addressed.

FIRE AND ICE

The temperature extremes of intense heat and extreme cold are useful in both nature and our visualizations.

Illustration 15: *Fire visualization:*
Flames engulfing your body

Illustration 16: *Lightning bolt visualization:*
A lightning bolt ripping through your nervous system

Fire

The fire visualization is very powerful and is used for the same purpose as it has in nature. It is a renewal force. It destroys the old and allows for fresh possibilities in the rebuilding of a new, healthy you.

Visualizing heat is useful for any problem, as the excessive heat attracts white blood cells to the area, and it is the white blood cells that will destroy the problem. It is a useful visualization for a tumor or cancer in one or more areas. It is also especially powerful to use when the problem is systemic—lymphoma, leukemia or a viral infection, for example—since you can visualize forcing steam through your entire circulatory system.

1. Imagine intensely hot flames roaring through your body. The force of the fire rips the problem from its roots.
2. Focus on the area where the problem exists. Some people find it easier to imagine being engulfed in flames (see Illustration 15).
3. Feel the heat and see the problem start to turn to ashes right before your eyes.

4. Incinerate the problem and watch it disintegrate. The ash blows away with the wind.

See the flames.
Feel the heat.
Hear the crackling.
Smell and taste the smoke in the air.
Make it real.

Another visualization using heat is that of the whistling kettle. It may help to have a whistling kettle in the background when you first try this visualization.

1. Imagine a whistling kettle at the location where you require healing. The steam is released with great, screaming force.
2. The heat from the steam is a focused stream of heat.
3. Allow the circulation of its heat all around the problem areas, and see the energy blockages dissipate.

See the steam rise.
Feel the heat.
Hear the whistle.
Smell and taste the vapors.
Make it real.

Ice

Just as fire is a very powerful force in nature, so is ice. It too destroys the old and allows for new growth potential in its wake. With the ice visualization, the life force of the problem can be frozen and then shattered, and so is useful for problems such as tumors.

1. Imagine the problem area freezing over.
2. See the cold, blue ice form as if liquid nitrogen were flowing over it.
3. Visualize this icy image shattering or melting away the problem.

See the problem freeze.
Feel the intense cold.
Hear the cracking of the ice.

Smell and taste the frigid, pristine air.
Make it real.

LIGHTNING BOLTS

This visualization is effective for any neurological disorder, such as multiple sclerosis, motor neuron disease and peripheral neuropathy. It is also very useful for pain from injuries, arthritis and fibromyalgia, as it seems to overload the nervous system, forcing it to reboot. You can apply this to any area or organ requiring stimulation. That part of the body then has to start up again fresh and new, since it has been reset to its healthy state. The new you emerges.

In this visualization, lightning does strike the same location again and again.

1. Imagine that a lightning bolt strikes the top of your head.
2. It rips through your body, lighting up your entire nervous system with laser precision (see Illustration 16).
3. All the synapses of your brain fire off, sending

intense pulses of energy down your spine, branching out until they reach the smallest nerve endings.

See the intense light of the lightning bolt.
Feel the energy ripping through you.
Hear its thunder.
Smell and taste its electrical charge.
Make it real.

SMART ENERGY PACKETS (SEPs)

Smart energy packets, or SEPs, are useful for removing a specific and localized problem. Visualize Pacman-like units circulating throughout your problem area. They orbit like swarming bees in a seek-and-destroy mission, yet spread healing energy in their path.

SEPs orbit and take a bite out of the problem, ingest it and then eliminate it from your system. It may help to visualize them as being Velcro-coated: As they make contact with the problem, they adhere to it. Removal is accomplished through exhaling (if it is a lung problem) or elimination of bodily waste

Illustration 17: *Smart energy packets visualization:*
SEPs orbiting the problem

Illustration 18: *Explosion visualization:*
Energy rippling out from the explosion site
as fragments of the problem vaporize

for other issues. This stick-and-remove approach is easy to visualize.

SEPs also reproduce themselves and communicate with each other. This ability is useful, as they can send signals to each other to shock or jump-start the system. They continue to be effective long after you do your visualization.

You may want to make this visualization more realistic by turning the SEPs into white blood cells. Attract them to your area of need. Visualize all the arteries and other blood vessels in your body becoming more permeable to white blood cells. This allows and encourages them to surround what needs to be removed from your body.

1. Imagine a swarm of SEPs orbiting through your energy blockage area (see Illustration 17).
2. Allow them to stick and grab onto the energy blockage in order to remove it from your body.
3. Allow the SEPs with the problem adhering to it to exit your body, and clean SEPs to enter your body.

See the smart energy packets orbiting.
Feel them sticking to the problem.
Hear them buzzing as they do their work.
Smell and taste the energy they are creating.
Make it real.

EXPLOSION

This is a powerful visualization for energetically ripping any problem out of your system. It can be used for anything from cancer to a stomach ache. For the best results, you need to visualize your problem as accurately as possible. Be your own health advocate and do the research required. Become familiar with its size, shape and location. The more detail you know, the more accurately you will be able to plant the explosive device in the most effective place. For those people who play computer games, it might help to imagine playing a game in which your health problem is the target.

1. Imagine that you are able to blast your problem out of your body.

Illustration 19:
Waterfall visualization:
Liquid energy pouring over your body

2. Plant the explosive device right in the center of your problem.

3. The explosion sends ripples of energy out from the epicenter. All fragments of the problem are instantly vaporized. (See Illustration 18.)

See the explosion.
Feel the vibration of the blast.
Hear the boom.
Smell and taste the burning matter.
Make it real.

WATERFALL

In this visualization, bluish-white liquid light energy cools, refreshes and cleanses your entire being. This visualization purifies you, and its intensity removes energy blocks, allowing you to exit the pattern of the injury or illness by overloading it. You automatically reboot; this is necessary to reset the system to your desired pattern of health.

1. Relax and imagine that you are standing under

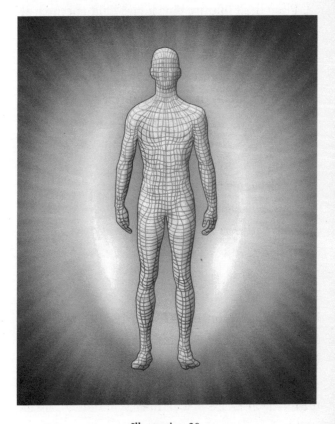

Illustration 20:
Patterned energy grid visualization:
A three-dimensional grid in the shape of your body

a waterfall of pure blue liquid light energy (see Illustration 19).

2. The energy is not only pouring over you but through you as it purifies. Its steady rhythm is soothing and relaxing, and it resets you.

3. Let the energy remove everything that it needs to in order to restore your health.

See the electric blue liquid light energy.
Feel it flowing through you.
Hear it cascading.
Smell and taste its refreshing qualities.
Make it real.

HOLDING YOUR STATE OF WELLNESS IN PLACE: THE PATTERNED ENERGY GRID

The waterfall visualization allows your energy to flow harmoniously in your new patterned energy grid. When you are in your optimum state of health, use the energy grid to hold it in place. This visualization can be done anytime—whether you are sitting on a bus or standing in an elevator. Your mind controls your body, and you control your mind. So work on keeping your mind-body healthy. We all have a perfect blueprint within us of our ideal health. Access it and hold it.

1. Visualize a three-dimensional grid in the shape of your body. The vertical and horizontal lines are perfectly spaced, or equidistant apart (see Illustration 20).
2. All your energy is flowing rhythmically, smoothly and harmoniously along these lines.

Through this visualization, the energy grid will hold your state of wellness.

WHEN AND WHERE TO DO VISUALIZATIONS

The best time to do these visualizations is right before bedtime; this is when they will be most effective. Keep doing them until you are too tired to continue. You'll drift off to sleep with your goals in focus. In your dream state, you are closest to the most effective state of consciousness for healing. You will heal at a phenomenal rate in your sleep.

You can also practice the visualizations throughout the day, aiming to integrate them into your daily routine. How long the visualizations should be done each time varies from person to person. Do them for as long as you can stay focused. This too varies from person to person. Most people are able to comfortably concentrate on them for about thirty minutes. Find a quiet location where you can relax and focus undisturbed.

If you find negative thoughts entering your mind, stop what you are doing, refocus and then start the visualization again. Through this repetitive exercise, you train your subconscious to be more aligned with your conscious thoughts. Over time, you will find that this becomes a natural process and that your positive thoughts have become more prominent.

Your goal is to do these visualizations until you are eventually having dreams about them. This is incredibly effective. Be a dreamhealer.

CUSTOMIZING THE GENERAL VISUALIZATIONS

The general visualizations I've outlined above are

to be used as guides only. You should experiment with them to find what works well for you. For instance, if you find that the lightning bolt visualization is too intense, change the color of light that you use. White light is the most intense, so color it blue or red and feel the difference. Turn down the amount of electricity that you are using. Change the color of the cloud that the strike originates from. The important point to remember is to be creative with your visualizations and be aware of their effect on you. Modify and customize these guides to suit your individual needs.

You say that the best time to visualize is before going to sleep, but I always fall asleep before I really have a chance to try them. What should I do?

It is likely that as you are drifting off, you have this book in hand and have set a visualization in your subconscious through your intention to do so. You may be unaware of the impact that this has on you. I would recommend that you not try so hard, as this process will eventually become a natural state for you. Relax and go with the flow. Keep it up as a habit, and you will notice the positive effects. Our dream state merges our subconscious instinctive thoughts with the conscious rational part of our minds to create a cinema-like action of reality. Your dreams will put into action your path to wellness.

I have a drinking problem. Could you recommend a visualization that would help me with this problem?
The visualizations for fatigue and emotional problems have also been helpful for lifestyle habits and addictions. By bringing lots of energy into yourself and redirecting it, you re-establish a harmonious flow. The tree root visualization for grounding I describe in Chapter 5 is also very useful in rebalancing energy, and many people find that it helps with emotional difficulties. Develop your own visualization specific to your challenge. You have already examined the triggers that lead you to drinking. Now visualize what it is that you need in order to quit. What is it that you are gaining by drinking? You know that you alone have the power to quit.

Chapter 9

Visualizations for Specific Conditions

Visualizations are only limited by our own imaginations.

—ADAM

$\mathcal{T}$ he specific visualizations I outline in this chapter can complement any treatment you may be undergoing through your doctor. These are visualizations that I have found to be effective for various conditions. There are many conditions that can affect, for instance, your respiratory system or your heart, so the first thing to do is see your doctor to determine which condition you have. The visualization strategies here incorporate very intensive and detailed information. While these skills are available to all, do not be surprised to discover that they will take a lot of practice before they are mastered. Many people have difficulty visualizing without precise instructions to follow. I want to emphasize that there is no wrong way to do these visualizations. You can use all the visualizations below, or you can use the ones you feel work best for you, or you can customize your visualization to be most effective for you or even create your own. It is up to you to try these various approaches and determine which are most effective for you. I do, however, suggest including certain anatomical facts to pinpoint the problem for your immune system. For instance, imagining attracting white blood cells to a cancerous tumor will make your visualization for cancer more effective than if you do not include actual anatomical features.

CANCER

Cancer occurs when cells become abnormal and continue to divide and form more cells, seemingly without order or control. Normally, cells divide to produce more cells only when the body needs them to maintain health. If cells continue to divide when new cells are not needed, a mass of tissue (a growth or tumor) forms.

Malignant tumors are cancerous. They can

invade and damage nearby tissues and organs. Cancer cells can break loose from a malignant tumor and travel through the bloodstream or the lymphatic system. This is how cancer can spread from the original tumor to form new tumors in other parts of the body.

Cancer usually develops gradually and is affected by factors related to lifestyle, environment and heredity. We can consciously diminish risk factors, since many cancers are related to smoking, diet and exposure to carcinogens in the environment. Some people are more sensitive than others to these risk factors. Inherited risk factors are unavoidable. We should be aware of them but know that not everyone with a particular risk for cancer actually gets the disease; in fact, most do not.

You can reduce your cancer risk by making some simple food choices. Eat a well-balanced diet made up of foods high in fiber, vitamins and minerals. Choose your foods wisely. Eat five servings of fruits and vegetables each day and a healthy amount of whole-grain breads and cereals.

Early on in my healing work, I observed some

interesting facts about cells, including cancer cells. I noticed that all cells communicate with each other. I see that, energetically, cancer is able to replicate quickly using what appears to be a sophisticated communications system. For example, when I use a particular visualization that works against one tumor, an adjacent tumor will not respond to the same visualization. It appears that the first tumor has warned the remaining tumors about the visualization. Through my connection and intuition I understand that this is happening.

The same mechanism that cancer cells use to send distress signals to other tumors can be used on cancer cells within a tumor to help destroy the tumor. When I did visualizations to break down communications within a tumor, the cancer cells passed on the message to all the cells in the tumor in a domino effect that was very useful in creating disorganization and disharmony within the cells of the tumor. I noticed that creating cell disorganization was more difficult when there were multiple tumors. I observed that as cancer begins to die, this communication between cancer cells slows down and eventually stops.

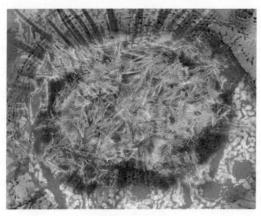

Illustration 21a:
Visualization for cancer:
Cancerous tumor

Illustration 21b:
Visualization for cancer:
White blood cells surrounding the tumor

When doing visualizations for any tumor, the goal is to weaken it and direct the immune system toward the tumor. Your body should have more than enough white blood cells to tackle any problem.

I find that the most effective method of getting at the cancer is by attacking it from as many angles as possible. Do research about your particular health challenge. Visualization techniques can be tailored to address individual lifestyle issues, including stress, attitudes, emotions, diet, exercise and your social environment.

As I mentioned above, it is helpful to include relevant anatomical facts in your visualization to pinpoint the problem for your immune system. For example, a useful visualization for cancer is imagining the attraction of white blood cells to the region of the tumor. Here's the most effective way to attract white blood cells to this area:

1. Imagine all the blood vessels in the vicinity of the tumor becoming more permeable to white blood cells. Allow white blood cells to exit the

Illustration 22a:
Visualization for cancer:
White blood cells destroying the tumor

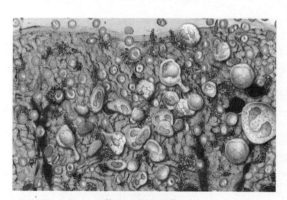

Illustration 22b:
Visualization for cancer:
Normal cells prevail; the tumor is gone

blood vessel walls and surround the tumor. Illustration 21 depicts how you might visualize the tumor, and then the white blood cells surrounding the tumor.

2. Visualize every white blood cell in your body being drawn to the tumor. Eventually, there should be so many white blood cells surrounding the tumor that they form a colony around it, completely engulfing it.

3. See the white blood cells that surround the tumor eating away at it. Essentially, the white blood cells grab the cancer cells, pull the cells inside them and then digest the cancer.

4. Visualize the white blood cells releasing substances that are poisonous to the cancer. See the tumor shriveling up from those toxins and from the white blood cells eating away at the tumor. (Note how detailed and physiologically precise these visualizations are.)

Illustration 22 shows first the white blood cells destroying the tumor, and then the area in the absence of the cancer cells.

The rate at which the white blood cells pick away at the cancer can vary. One factor is the temperature. The cells will eat away at the cancer at a far faster rate in warmer conditions. Therefore, you might also visualize flames raging underneath the tumor to apply heat to the area. Heat also increases the blood circulation, which speeds up the healing process.

A tumor needs nutrients to survive. Without a supply of fresh nutrients and without an exit mechanism for wastes, the tumor will die. Here's an effective visualization for this:

1. Visualize the blood vessels that supply nutrients to the tumor contracting to the point where there is no transfer of nutrients.
2. Visualize the tumor drowning in its own toxins and waste products. See this happen until the cancer cells simply die.
3. Visualize choking off what the cancer needs and simultaneously attacking it in order to weaken the cancer.
4. As the essential needs of the cancer are being

blocked, visualize the communication links between cells in the tumor (or between tumors) falling apart.

5. Once the communication links fail, visualize the cancer shrinking and losing its life energy as it becomes inactive.

6. Your body must now physically remove this tissue. Visualize a garbage disposal system working away 24–7 to remove the physical mass from your body.

LEUKEMIA

Leukemia is cancer of the white blood cells. These cancer cells are formed in the bone marrow—where all bloods cells are produced—and inhibit the production of normal white and red blood cells. The goal of any visualization for leukemia is to stimulate the bone marrow into producing a normal amount of red and white blood cells. Visualize lightning bolts going through the bone marrow one after the other until you can see a healthy number of red and white blood cells being formed. Keep doing this visualization throughout the session until you become confident in the process.

NEUROLOGICAL CONDITIONS

Neurologically based disorders include multiple sclerosis, fibromyalgia, chronic fatigue syndrome, head and spine traumas, central nervous system infections and growths, and peripheral nerve disorders.

I have held several workshops specifically for chronic fatigue syndrome and fibromyalgia, with great success. Many participants report that they no longer have these ailments, and many others note significant improvement in their quality of life.

Your nervous system has a direct effect on your immune system; therefore, virtually every health issue benefits from a positive change in your nervous system. Regardless of the health challenge you are facing, stimulating your nervous system will benefit you, whether you have an emotional or psychological issue or a physical problem. It is also useful in regaining physical energy, vitality and strength.

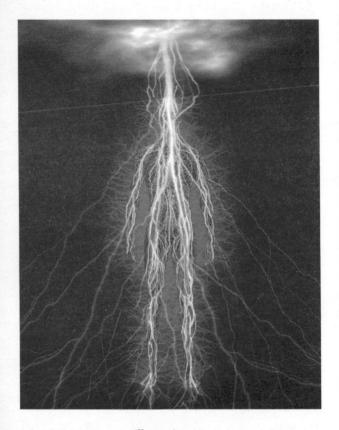

Illustration 23:
Visualization for neurological conditions:
Lightning bolts ripping through your nervous system

1. Visualize lightning bolts ripping through your entire nervous system (see Illustration 23). Remember that the goal of these lightning bolts is to reboot your nervous system.

2. Watch these bolts light up your nervous system, from your head, down your spine and to every nerve ending. After this "storm" passes, imagine calming ripples being emitted from your entire nervous system.

RESPIRATORY CONDITIONS

Many conditions can lead to breathing problems. Some issues, such as asthma, affect the air passages, while others, such as lung cancer, directly influence the function of the lungs. The first thing to do is see your doctor to determine which condition you have.

Asthma is a condition that makes it more difficult for you to breathe. When you inhale, air passes to your lungs through tubular airways called bronchi. When you have an asthma attack, the walls of these airways contract and become inflamed.

Factors that can trigger asthma attacks are

Illustration 24a:
Visualization for respiratory conditions:
Inhaling SEPs

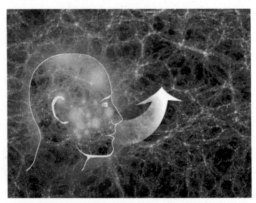

Illustration 24b:
Visualization for respiratory conditions:
Exhaling SEPs containing the debris

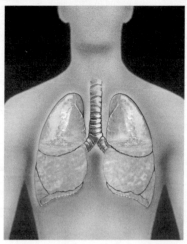

Illustration 25: *Visualization for respiratory conditions:* Lungs
soaking up liquid energy and expanding

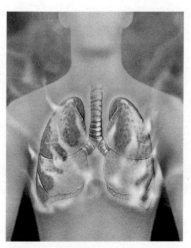

Illustration 26: *Visualization for respiratory conditions:*
A raging fire vaporizing your problem

smoke, dust, pollen, air pollution and allergies. Stress can make asthma worse. To me, asthma looks like a thick, sticky fog throughout the airways leading to the lungs. Lung problems often respond well to visualizations because there is so much circulation throughout the respiratory system. With this large amount of circulation in the lungs, the problem can exit the body rapidly. Most people with lung problems cough up a lot of phlegm after the treatments. Many people notice that breathing is easier and takes less effort. These differences are often noticeable quickly.

Smart energy packets, or SEPs, are helpful with respiratory conditions, as they can be breathed in directly to your problem site, where they stick to the problem like glue. They can then be eliminated on exhalation (see Illustration 24). To enhance the realism of the visualizations, feel the problem moving out of your lungs with every breath.

1. Imagine bluish liquid energy filling your lungs (see Illustration 25). If you have asthma, visualize your airways—your breathing tubes—expanding as they soak up this liquid energy.

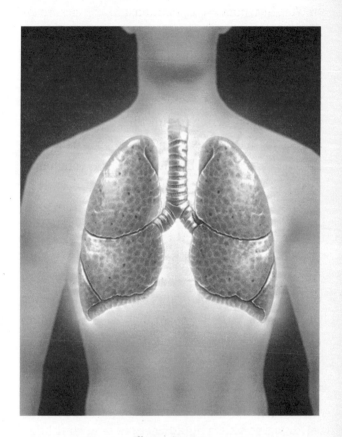

Illustration 27:
Visualization for respiratory conditions:
Clean lungs

2. Watch your tubes expand, just as sponges do when they soak up liquid. The problem is absorbed into this liquid, which then evaporates into glowing energy.

3. Take deep breaths and absorb all this energy as deeply as you can.

4. Visualize a raging bonfire with flames burning underneath your lungs. See your problem shrivel up, vaporized by the intense heat (see Illustration 26).

5. Once your problem is completely vaporized, begin to take deep breaths. Imagine taking a deep breath of energized air into your lungs. This energy is absorbed down to the cellular level.

6. See your smallest capillaries light up and reflect this energetic boost. Every airway is clear and bright.

7. On exhalation, watch more and more of the vapor leave your lungs until they are clean and are a pinkish color (see Illustration 27).

HEART CONDITIONS

There are many conditions that can affect your heart, so the first thing to do is see your doctor to determine which condition you have. The visualizations in this chapter can be done to complement any therapy, and you can modify them for your specific heart problem. Remember that there is no wrong way to do these visualizations. I am simply suggesting that you modify them to fit your diagnosis and therefore find what works best for you.

However, any heart problem is reflected in your breathing; this must be addressed:

1. Imagine breathing pure air so deeply into your lungs that it energizes the very functions of your cells.
2. Visualize this cellular impact of pure energy being absorbed by every fiber of your being. See every pathway being energized as all cells in your body bathe in this pure energy.

Blood Pressure Problems
(Hypertension or Hypotension)

Stress is a major factor in high blood pressure, so it is essential that you relax in a comfortable position to visualize. Stay away from clocks that may remind you of the passage of time, which may cause tension. This is your time for yourself. Use it wisely. For those with hypotension, the purpose of this visualization is to regulate your heart's pumping ability, so be sure to relax and focus on this objective.

1. Visualize your heart filling up with a calming, pure, glowing energy (see Illustration 28).
2. Once your heart is filled, watch the glowing energy get distributed more and more evenly throughout your body with every heartbeat. Watch the glowing energy spread down every artery and every vein until your entire circulatory system is filled with this calming energy. Every tiny capillary is energized.
3. Watch your heart rhythmically pumping, until your heartbeat is calm, relaxed and regular.

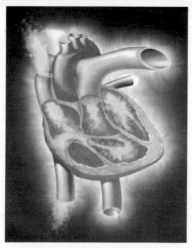

Illustration 28: *Visualization for heart conditions:* Glowing energy filling the heart

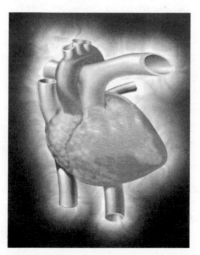

Illustration 29: *Visualization for heart conditions:* A calm, relaxed heart

Visualize calming ripples of energy emanating from your heart (see Illustration 29).
4. Breathe deeply, and enjoy feeling good.

When doing your visualizations, be creative. But do make sure that in the last step of each visualization for your heart, it is always beating at a relaxed yet steady rate. With each beat, feel the force behind each regular contraction.

INFECTIOUS DISEASES

Many infectious diseases, including AIDS, HIV, hepatitis, cold and flu, are spread throughout the body. SEPs are a useful visualization tool for these types of ailments (see Chapter 8).

1. Visualize SEPs or white blood cells dispersing themselves throughout your entire body, engulfing the problem (bacteria or virus) cell by cell (see Illustration 30).
2. Visualize white blood cells permeating the blood vessel walls in great numbers, totally

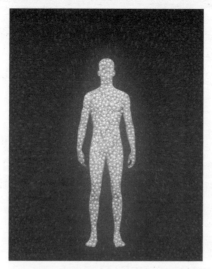

Illustration 30: *Visualization for infectious diseases:*
SEPs dispersed throughout the body

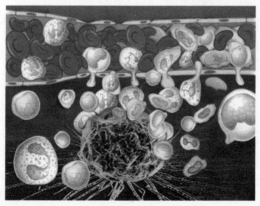

Illustration 31: *Visualization for infectious diseases:*
White blood cells attacking the problem

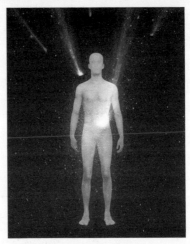

Illustration 32: *Visualization for infectious diseases:* Localized explosion

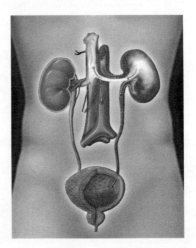

Illustration 33: *Visualization for infectious diseases:* Kidneys filtering out dirty blood

engulfing a localized problem area (see Illustration 31).

3. Visualize explosions in a specific area to address any localized problem. Think of comets or asteroids hitting where this is needed (see Illustration 32).

4. Visualize your kidneys filtering everything out of the dirty blood, or blood that contains the now inactive bacteria or viruses (see Illustration 33). Continue the visualization until only clean blood is going in and coming out of your kidneys, and white blood cells no longer have anything to "eat."

GASTROINTESTINAL CONDITIONS

Emotional issues and stress often aggravate gastrointestinal issues. Take time out to relax and visualize. One way to accomplish this is to sit down with a cup of green or caffeine-free tea before starting. Take a sip and move your awareness with the soothingly warm liquid. Be mindful of its calming effect.

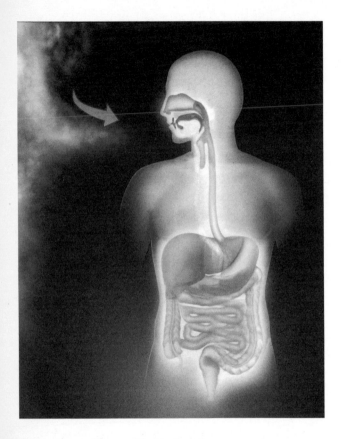

Illustration 34:
Visualization for gastrointestinal conditions:
Digestive tract absorbing pure energy

1. Visualize pure light energy being absorbed all along your digestive tract (see Illustration 34).
2. See the unobstructed flow through your body from your mouth, esophagus, stomach, small intestine, large intestine and colon, and flushing out as waste.
3. See your entire digestive system working perfectly. Calming ripples of energy radiate throughout your system, nourishing every cell in its path.

PAIN ISSUES

Sometimes it seems as though there are as many different causes of pain as there are people living with it. Typically, mainstream Western medicine manages pain issues with drugs, rather than getting to the root cause. Visualizations vary depending on the source of the pain.

1. Imagine breathing in pure, warm sunshine energy deep within your lungs and heart area.
2. Form a concentrated ball of energy in the painful area.

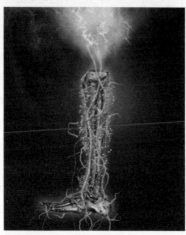

Illustration 35: *Visualization for joint conditions:* Lightning bolt moving throughout the joint

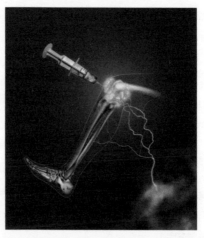

Illustration 36: *Visualization for joint conditions:* A needle dispensing white liquid energy

3. Visualize this ball picking up pieces of pain like lint and radiating it out of your body in the form of sunshine. The warm rays carry with them everything that needs to leave your body. In its place is left glowing radiance. Feels good, doesn't it?

JOINT CONDITIONS, CHRONIC AND ACUTE

These visualizations are for any condition related to joints or mobility problems. Remember, you have the power to improvise your own visualizations.

The general visualization using lightning bolts (see Chapter 8) is helpful to many people.

1. Visualize lightning bolts forcefully moving throughout your joint until it is healed (see Illustration 35).
2. Imagine injecting a needle into your joint, dispensing a white liquid energy that totally surrounds all moving parts (see Illustration 36). This white liquid energy acts as lubrication for your joint.

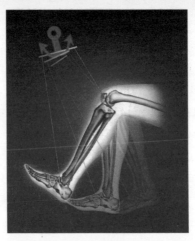

Illustration 37: *Visualization for joint conditions:*
Support wires holding your joint in place
as you test your range of motion

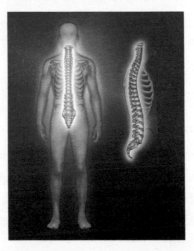

Illustration 38: *Visualization for back injuries:*
A glowing, white, malleable rod
running through your spine

3. Visualize gently testing the mobility of your joint by imagining many support wires at different angles holding your joint in place (see Illustration 37). Each wire adds support to various parts of your joint, and moves the joint or limb around like the strings of a marionette. Test your range of motion by playing in your mind's eye a sport you once enjoyed. Remember how wonderful it is to feel the breeze against your face as you hike, bike, play tennis or golf. As the mobility of the joint is being tested in your mind's eye, there is no pain at all. There is not even the thought of pain present. Remember how this feels and recall it often.

BACK INJURIES

Back injuries are very common. In group treatments this area is always addressed, as I haven't held one yet where this hasn't been an issue for many participants. Depending on the nature of your injury, it might be difficult to even get comfortable for a visualization session, but do your best.

1. Visualize a glowing white malleable rod going through the middle of your spine (see Illustration 38). This rod acts as a support.

2. Imagine that with every inhalation you are filling your lungs with pure energy. Create an energy flow from the top of your head through your spine and out through your tailbone. Visualize this pathway lighting up like a neon sign.

3. Visualize supporting your back while you are moving it around with great flexibility. The range of motion of your back is being tested through your imagery. There should be no painful sensation or even the thought of pain.

4. Visualize your back cracking into place as if in a chiropractic procedure. Your back is being reset to its optimum position.

5. In your visualization, flex your back to test its full range of motion until you have a secure sense of stability. Reach your comfort zone. You should then see yourself doing all the normal movements that have not been possible until now because of your back problem. See

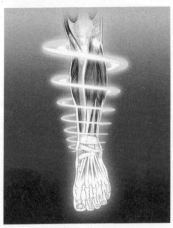

Illustration 39: *Visualization for muscle injuries:*
Spiral of energy surrounding the injured muscle

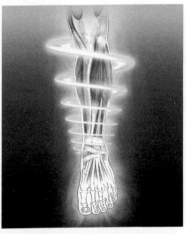

Illustration 40: *Visualization for muscle injuries:*
Glowing energy bathes the muscle

yourself doing these things with no pain or discomfort whatsoever.

As you experiment with your visualizations, continue to modify and develop those that work best for you.

MUSCLE INJURIES

Even if it is difficult to loosen up because of the pain, you must try to get in a relaxing position for your visualization session. Take a deep breath and begin.

1. Visualize a white spiral of calming liquid energy surrounding the problem area (see Illustration 39). See all your muscles soak up the liquid like a sponge.
2. Once your muscles become completely saturated with this liquid energy, watch calming waves of electrical pulses ripple out from your muscle. Feel the muscles relax as they bathe in the glowing energy (see Illustration 40).

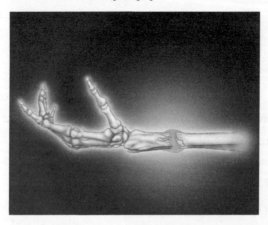

Illustration 41: *Visualization for broken bones:*
The area of your fracture absorbing bright white light

Illustration 42: *Visualization for broken bones:* Energy radiating outward as you flood the area with warm light

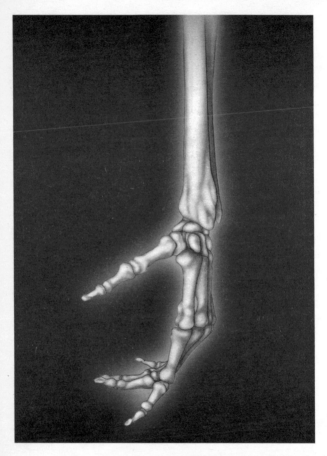

Illustration 43:
Visualization for broken bones:
The fracture as healed

BROKEN BONES

Most fractures need to be physically set by a doctor first. The following visualization is intended to speed up your recovery. This visualization involves heat, which dramatically increases the rate at which every chemical reaction takes place, allowing an increase in blood circulation. This speeds up the healing process.

With multiple fractures, you can either do this visualization on one fracture at a time, or you can visualize healing the entire bone at once. Again, use whatever works best for you. There are no firm rules for what will work and what will not, as any visualization will direct the immune system to some degree.

1. Visualize a bright white light being absorbed into and then emitted from the inside of your bone (see Illustration 41). This bright light creates heat.
2. Imagine wrapping energy around your fracture.
3. Energy radiates outward as you flood the entire area with warm, healing light to speed

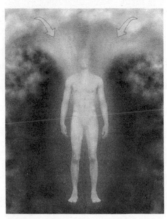

Illustration 44: *Visualization for fatigue and emotional problems:* Pulling all the energy in the universe into yourself through the top of your head

Illustration 45: *Visualization for fatigue and emotional problems:* Your abundant energy exploding outward in all directions

up the mending process (see Illustration 42). Watch new healthy bone filling in any breaks, until there is no longer any sign of there ever having been a problem. Visualize the fracture as completely healed (see Illustration 43).

FATIGUE AND EMOTIONAL PROBLEMS

Emotional problems weigh heavy on our minds and this uses up a lot of our energy. By taking an emotional load off, we will feel lighter and have more energy to enjoy life. Bringing in energy helps accomplish this task. You may want to customize your visualization by seeing yourself actually taking that load off your back.

The visualization for fatigue or emotional problems is similar to the technique used to expand auras, as described in Chapter 2, "Bring in Universal Energy." Do this visualization whenever you feel exhausted and are in need of an energy booster. I have found this to be an effective tool in regaining energy after an intense workout. It is also effective in increasing the maximum amount of exercise you can do within your comfort zone. For example, I use this to increase the amount of weight that I can lift when working out in the weight room.

1. Visualize all the energy in the universe being pulled into you (see Illustration 44). Continue absorbing all this energy until you feel that your energy system is completely saturated. Mastering this takes practice.
2. Once all the energy is within you, imagine that it powerfully explodes in all directions (see Illustration 45). The shock wave of energy ripples out. When this has disappeared from sight, all that is left is a clear, pure white hologram of yourself, with no sign whatsoever of any problem.

Another effective visualization is of sending streams of laser light to loosen the knot that is holding you back from doing what it is that you want to do. Set yourself free.

CUSTOMIZING YOUR VISUALIZATIONS

It would be an impossible task to address in detail

every possible visualization applicable to every ailment known. Not only is it unrealistic but it is unnecessary, as you hold the key to all visualizations. It is called imagination.

Be creative. Change or customize the visualization to suit you. Never underestimate your own power in your health and healing. Visualizations are a tool for you to use. Your response to them is an individual process. So is what works most effectively for you. Some readers may have read this entire book and still be wondering, "Which visualization is the correct one for my condition?" If this is you, ask yourself these questions:

1. Have I researched my ailment as thoroughly as I am able to?
2. Do I know what the proper and healthy functioning of this area should be?
3. Do I know what this area should look like?
4. Have I practiced the general visualizations and varied them according to my specific challenge?
5. Have I practiced the specific visualizations

that are most relevant for me and modified them accordingly?

All the visualizations in this book are designed to make you feel more comfortable as you explore what works most effectively for you. Becoming comfortable with yourself is the most important step toward self-empowerment. Trust yourself on your way forward.

Conclusion

If the material in this book has helped even one person with his or her healing journey, it has in fact helped us all. What appears to separate us is only an illusion. What we do for ourselves is ultimately what we do for everyone. Helping everyone is an unavoidable outcome of truly helping ourselves.

Stay tuned!

DreamHealer

For information about workshops,
newsletters and ordering the DVD

DreamHealer Visualizations of Self-Empowerment

visit **www.dreamhealer.com**

DreamHealer

A True Story of Miracle Healings

Adam has an extraordinary gift: he is credited with healing thousands of people around the world. This is his astonishing, true story . . .

To his friends he is just Adam. But in the world of alternative healing, he is fast becoming the most talked-about energy healer alive today.

Growing up in Canada, Adam quickly realised that he was different from other children, for he had an extraordinary gift. He could look at a person and see the energy inside their body, and he gradually learned how to control and manipulate this energy to ease pain.

DreamHealer tells of how Adam treated his mother for MS when he was just fourteen; of healing himself when he fractured his spine in a swimming accident; and of helping many other people who share their stories in this book.

Now, at the age of 19, he has the unique ability to connect to and influence another person's health from a distance. Whether or not they are on the same continent as he is makes no difference. In *DreamHealer*, Adam shares his thoughts, observations and wisdom for the first time, including the seven steps every reader can take today to improve their health and well-being.

DreamHealer 3

The Quantum World of Energy Healing

Adam has healed many people and helped many people with the healing of themselves: his mother's MS when he was 14, himself when he fractured his spine and many other people who share their stories in the book. At his popular workshops held throughout North America, he teaches people how to effectively focus their own healing intentions for self-empowerment. His unique group treatments, which involve all attendees, are the highlight of these events.

In *DreamHealer 3*, Adam shares his thoughts, observations and wisdom that is often far beyond his years. He describes how the mysteries of healing are connected with science and spirituality as one.

Other bestselling titles available by mail:

☐ Dreamhealer   Adam   £6.99

The prices shown above are correct at time of going to press. However, the publishers reserve the right to increase prices on covers from those previously advertised without further notice.

───────────── sphere ─────────────

SPHERE
PO Box 121, Kettering, Northants NN14 4ZQ
Tel: 01832 737525, Fax: 01832 733076
Email: aspenhouse@FSBDial.co.uk

POST AND PACKING:
Payments can be made as follows: cheque, postal order (payable to Sphere), credit card or Switch Card. Do not send cash or currency.

All UK Orders	**FREE OF CHARGE**
EC & Overseas	25% of order value

Name (BLOCK LETTERS) . . . .

Address . . . .

. . . .

Post/zip code: . . . .

☐ Please keep me in touch with future Sphere publications

☐ I enclose my remittance £ . . . .

☐ I wish to pay by Visa/Access/Mastercard/Eurocard/Switch Card

Card Expiry Date ☐☐☐☐   Switch Issue No. ☐☐